Early Years Education and Care

What are the new benchmarks for the future in good early years provision? What should children and parents expect from practice given recent research evidence on how young children thrive?

Developing and managing early years provision has changed significantly over the last few years. Parental expectations, policy creep, bureaucracy overload, inadequate training, a litigious climate, over-dependence on screens, traffic danger and child protection anxiety are among the many challenges now faced by early years providers. This timely new book explores the key issues faced by settings and what they mean for early years practice.

Looking at the real evidence around children's learning and well-being, parental preference and social trends, the book covers:

- neuro-scientific research into the way children learn

- what parents know and expect

- children's well-being

- the indoor and outdoor environment

- adult intervention

- the risk/benefit equation

- nutrition, health and exercise.

Drawing on examples of outstanding practice from a wide range of settings, this exciting new book will help practitioners reach beyond what is expected and provide the very best for the children in their care.

Susan Hay was previously Executive Director Europe for Bright Horizons Family Solutions, an international group of nurseries operating in the US, the UK, Canada and Ireland. She is currently a freelance consultant.

Early Years Education and Care

New issues for practice from research

Edited by Susan Hay

Routledge
Taylor & Francis Group

LONDON AND NEW YORK

First published 2015
by Routledge
2 Park Square, Milton Park, Abingdon, Oxon OX14 4RN

and by Routledge
711 Third Avenue, New York, NY 10017

Routledge is an imprint of the Taylor & Francis Group, an informa business

© 2015 Susan Hay

The right of the editor to be identified as the author of the editorial material, and of the authors for their individual chapters, has been asserted in accordance with sections 77 and 78 of the Copyright, Designs and Patents Act 1988.

British Library Cataloguing in Publication Data
A catalogue record for this book is available from the British Library

Library of Congress Cataloging in Publication Data
Early years education and care : new issues for practice from research / edited by Susan Hay.
        pages cm
    1. Early childhood education—Great Britain.   2. Child care—Great Britain.
    3. Child development.   I. Hay, Susan, 1951–
    LB1139.3.G7E269 2014
    372.210941—dc23   2014024112

ISBN: 978-1-138-78344-7 (hbk)
ISBN: 978-1-138-78345-4 (pbk)
ISBN: 978-1-315-76870-0 (ebk)

Typeset in Celeste
by Keystroke, Station Road, Codsall, Wolverhampton

For Cecily,
who begins her nursery career as this goes to press

Contents

Contents

Figures

Figures

Foreword

There is general agreement on the importance of the early years, increasingly supported by rigorous evidence, and shared across all political parties in the UK. As contributors to this book show, providers of high quality care and education who pay attention to children as individuals and reach out to parents can make a significant difference to children's life chances. There can be no better investment for society as a whole.

Susan Hay is recognised as an effective, influential and principled manager of leading services of excellent early years provision, built up during a period of rapid change and development in the UK. Drawing on her experience, she has assembled an influential group of experts, whose informed contributions cover the multi-faceted field of early years care and education. Their insights coupled with her editorial comments provide a comprehensive overview of a complex topic.

The differing perspectives highlight the need for providers to keep in mind the enduring principles that inform all effective work in this field, while remaining alert to new trends and possibilities. We are reminded of the prime importance of a nurturing and responsive social environment that promotes consistent and reliable attachment to significant adults, and of sensitively handled transitions that take account of individual personalities. Play, including access to outdoor environments and elements of manageable risk, is the key to intellectual as well as physical and social development and the disposition to pursue learning. Adults can discover more about young children's interests and abilities through observing them in open-ended activities than through predetermined tests.

A common thread throughout the book is a concern for children's well-being. The increasing emphasis in the UK on future economic success coupled with the promotion of childcare as a means of getting parents back to work undermines the perception of early education as an intrinsic good, so the clear message that the most important aspect of accountability is to children's welfare and secure progress is welcome.

This is accompanied by an acknowledgement of the importance of staff qualifications, supported by overwhelming international evidence that the quality and effectiveness of provision depends on professional training and good leadership. Since the home learning environment has the greatest influence on outcomes for children, part of the role of staff must be outreach to families. One factor that differentiates more effective provision is the degree to which staff include parents as partners and provide help with home experiences that can promote children's learning, such as responsive communication and opportunities for open-ended play.

Another indicator of quality is the relationship between nurseries and schools, which is particularly important in the UK where the school starting age is comparatively young. The Early Years Foundation Stage bridges the two sectors, and it is vital that downward pressures from more formal approaches are not allowed to distort practice. Indeed, children who do not reach a good level of development as measured by the Early Years Profile should arguably be entitled to provision in Year 1 that continues the approach required in the Foundation Stage. There are particular dangers in arbitrary expected standards that are not developmentally appropriate and in a limited and limiting view of school readiness.

Other current issues, such as the funded provision for disadvantaged two year olds which is aimed at narrowing the gap of achievement between children from disadvantaged families and others, or trends towards deregulation, for example of staff qualifications and ratios, separate space for rest, and access to outdoors, are not explicitly addressed, but providers are encouraged to stay abreast of developments and to resist potentially damaging developments as well as looking out for opportunities for improvement.

Professor Melhuish points out that improving life chances in early childhood can serve both the goals of reducing inequality and raising productive capacity. He observes that it is relatively straightforward to legislate for early childhood care and education, but difficult in a democratic society to legislate for parenting. However, as Susan Hay explains, mutually supportive and constructive partnerships between early years providers and parents, mediated by key staff, can create a virtual cycle of raised understanding and aspiration.

The core messages of this book are motivating, timely and highly relevant. They promote the professional awareness of managers and staff across all services involved in early years work, who have a significant contribution to make to the future as well as the present of individual children and their families, and to wider society.

Wendy Scott
April 2014

Introduction

Susan Hay

Many aspects of developing and managing early years provision have changed over the last few years as a result of significant shifts in public policy, the regulatory framework, training for early years professionals, brain research, environmental developments, parental concerns and the investment climate.

Staff arrive with different training than in the past and the Ofsted quality regime is familiar to both professionals and parents. The knowledge required to develop and manage services within this framework is then readily available in this landscape of 'givens'. The question is whether the framework is sufficiently agile to incorporate and learn from what research tells us, and what society demands of the multi-layered endeavour of educating and caring for our youngest children.

My purpose is to turn the lens onto the issues that lie beyond standard training, regulation and inspection, and think about the entitlements that young children have, and the expectations that parents can reasonably anticipate, in services now, given the externally driven influences of the latest research, the current societal climate and extra-curricular trends which are now making themselves present. This book is for all those thinking about, reviewing and making decisions about the service they really want to provide: what values do they want to espouse and what will their 'cutting edge' look like within the highly competitive and standardised landscape of school-based and centre-based early years provision now?

I have tried to bring this new knowledge together and demonstrate different responses to each of the issues through carefully selected, independently authored chapters. In some cases, it is early years practice that has led others to evaluate and adapt their service to remain relevant; in others it has been research that has driven change.

Why are these new issues relevant, where did they come from, and why should we take account of them now? We discuss them from the perspective of diverse young children's settings and sectors, from research institutions and from contemporary thinkers, drawing on good practice as well as contemporary thought and authoritative research to demonstrate how we could embrace what we know now and update our work.

Early years services have become highly regulated through the developing Ofsted inspection regime and standardised across all settings over the past few years. This has resulted in there being little difference in the basic requirements of, or services provided by, the numerous different settings in which young children find themselves. Another major shift has been the focus on training and professionalisation of early years staff, and the introduction of early years teachers into settings that did not attract them before. Thirdly, parental leave has been extended as of legal right, and as a corporate benefit as companies compete for staff, which has changed the demand for and shape of childcare provision.

These three separate but connected initiatives have driven new research, knowledge and experience in both the early years curriculum and its management, previously the territory of optional continuing professional development, but now mainstreamed as part of leadership training. To offer a service that reaches beyond what is expected as basic now and which is at the fingertips of all the constituent parties – parents, managers, regulators – and one that exceeds regular and recognised standards and meets what we actually know matches the needs of children, as well as the contemporary expectations of parents, and that demonstrates new value and excellence, providers must embrace multiple external sources of information, learning and inspiration. The sector must not allow itself to be confined by its own, required experience.

The following chapters look at the issues emerging from research and practice, which have not always been prefaced with an early years tag, that need to form part of every service in the future for it to remain relevant. Issues such as:

- how health and education, from a policy perspective, are increasingly coming together;

- the latest neuro-scientific research into the way children learn;

- how children are maturing earlier and what this means for services;
- how to serve the increase in families with only one child;
- our concern with nutrition and exercise as a counter to obesity;
- recognition and realisation of the importance of the environment in which children live;
- re-connecting children with nature;
- our concern for children's long-term well-being and happiness;
- screen life;
- risk 'benefits', rather than risk 'assessments';
- time poverty of parents;
- visible social and community responsibility values.

The chapter authors have been drawn from widely-respected research organisations or are recognised practice experts. Sharing what they know and relating it to your service, they offer answers to the questions: What are the new benchmarks for future excellence in early years provision? What are the conditions and parameters within which the values of the service offered become visible and within which practice can thrive? How can school be inspired to be ready for children who have experienced good early years services?

The contributors are:

Ian Frampton

Ian is a Consultant in Paediatric Psychology, and a Senior Lecturer at the European Centre for Environment and Human Health (ECEHH) at the University of Exeter Medical School, based in Cornwall. He has also worked with children with neurodevelopmental disabilities in early years settings.

Philip Gammage

Emeritus Professor Philip Gammage has been a primary teacher, academic and civil servant involved in education for the last fifty years. He was President of BAECE and Chair of TACTYC, held the Chair and Deanship at Nottingham University and has worked in twenty-one countries. Philip was involved in the OECD assessment of early childhood education and care in Finland and has regularly taught EC classes there over the last fifteen years. He holds an honorary doctorate from Oulu University for services to education. He also teaches regularly in Australia, where he was for five years Adviser to the South Australian Minister.

Susan Hay

Having worked in planning and architecture, Susan's principal career has been in the development of employer-sponsored work life and childcare solutions in the UK, becoming Executive Chairman of Bright Horizons Family Solutions in Europe, 2000–2006. She acted as an adviser to successive government, academic and campaigning working parties on the economics of childcare provision, childcare environments and the quality of services. Susan is a past Chair of Working Families and past Chair of Governors for a primary school in London. More recently, Susan has become a patient advocate for children with cancer, leading several charities and working with the National Institute for Clinical Excellence (NICE) on earlier diagnosis.

Helen Huleatt

Helen's parents were among the founders of Community Playthings in the United States shortly after the Second World War. Following a childhood immersed in Froebel's ethos, Helen trained in early years in the 1970s. After five years of working with children she joined the Community Playthings business where she has worked for fifteen years.

Rebecca Jenkin

Rebecca is a Child Psychology Researcher at the European Centre for Environment and Human Health.

Sonia Mainstone-Cotton

Sonia is a senior project worker and trainer with The Children's Society, specialising in participation work with under-fives. Sonia first joined The Children's Society in 1994. Sonia has an MA in Early Childhood Studies.

Edward Melhuish

Edward Melhuish is Professor of Human Development at Birkbeck, University of London and Visiting Professorial Fellow at the Institute of Education, University of London. He was a Principal Investigator of studies of day care and family life in the 1980s, and has conducted research on child development, parenting and childcare on behalf of the European Commission. He was Principal Investigator on the Effective Provision of Pre-school Education (EPPE) and the Executive Director of the National Evaluation of Sure Start.

Mark Miller
Mark trained as an early years teacher at Goldsmiths College, University of London, at the end of the 1970s, and is currently Headteacher at Robert Blair Primary School, London Borough of Islington. Earlier in his career he was Head of Early Years and Childcare in a local authority in south London. Mark is also involved in training the next generation of teachers as a tutor on a local 'Schools Direct' programme.

Larissa Pople
Larissa is a Senior Researcher at The Children's Society, leading on their children's well-being and child poverty research programmes. She first joined The Children's Society in 2006, and has also worked at UNICEF UK and on the Independent Commission on Youth Crime and Antisocial Behaviour.

Wendy Scott
Wendy is a Froebel-trained teacher with wide experience including work in the private, voluntary and independent sector as well as early years classes in disadvantaged parts of London and rural areas. Headship of a demonstration nursery school was followed by a year as Principal Lecturer in Early Years, where she coordinated an advanced diploma in multi-professional studies. Inspection experience with the ILEA and the Royal Borough of Kensington and Chelsea was followed by time with Ofsted as a Registered Inspector and trainer. As a former Chief Executive of the British Association for Early Childhood Education, and Chair of the Early Childhood Forum, Wendy served as an adviser with the DfEE on Sure Start and the Early Excellence programme. She has worked on early years development with the British Council in China and with UNICEF in the Maldives. She is currently President of TACTYC (Association for the Development of Early Years Teachers), and recently served on the expert panel involved in Professor Nutbrown's Review of Qualifications for the early years.

Philip Waters
Philip is a Play Specialist Researcher at the European Centre for Environment and Human Health.

The book is arranged in two broad sections that look at:

1 Service values and principles.

2 Making values visible.

The authors all consider their work to be in progress, and arguably it will never finish. That is my point: today's excellence is only tomorrow's standard, so we must never rest on our laurels, even if we have been rated as outstanding. Let's call it 'future proofing'.

Section 1 starts with a review of what the huge changes in regulation and research over the last decade mean for practice, and goes on to discuss:

- the context in which practice takes place today;

- the environments in which young children find themselves;

- the long-term consequences of early childhood education and parenting;

- the new perceptions and expectations parents have of early childhood education;

- what we know now about children's well-being.

Section 2 looks at how services can embrace the latest research and offer authority to practices within the context of a multi-faceted landscape of environments:

- early years practice in the school setting;

- making the indoor environment work for children;

- benefits of the outdoor environment;

- making use of research in practice.

Some of the issues addressed, from both a research perspective and how they play out in everyday practice, through these chapters are:

- learning from neuroscience, politics and policy;

- learning from longitudinal studies as practitioners, as parents and as policy makers;

- applying research findings to daily life;

- the right to be listened to as a child;

- critical concepts of well-being;

- measuring well-being and how this informs practice;

- aspirations and expectations of parents;

- the skills and expertise with which children come to early years settings now, and how settings build on these;

- handling, nurturing and developing children accustomed to a play-based individualised curriculum in school, and how school adapts to children transferring from under-fives settings;

- engaging parents at this early education stage;

- creating the environment to allow children to thrive;

- complementing home life;

- connection with nature and the community;

- the risk/benefit equation;

- the challenge of screen life;

- analysing the adult's attitude and role;

- accountability and predictors of success;

- education and health in tandem.

The political attitude towards childcare provision does not differ substantially along party lines, and the economic outlook is forecast to remain fairly stable. It is therefore unlikely that there will be change within the sector of the dramatic, public policy nature we have seen over the past few years, in the foreseeable future. Public funding will go up and down but within the limits that voters can tolerate. The critical thread throughout the book is the need to remain agile to research, to parental preferences, and to social trends. These are the constituencies that should be leading practice; practice should not wait for a regulatory framework to change (which generally only catches up with best practice) before reviewing the service offered. It is this attitude, of looking through several lenses at the same time and keeping professional antennae alive for inspiration, which I hope these contributions get across. Although the issues may change, this purpose will continue to be relevant whilst we have a mixed – and increasingly competitive – economy of early years provision.

Service values and principles

Early childhood education and care in context

Philip Gammage

Introduction

The provision of early childhood education and care (ECEC) is a major preoccupation of most advanced nations. Certainly the thirty-four (2014) OECD member countries have remarkably close agreement over its importance. However, policy makers (usually politicians), the public and the professionals are often not agreed on purpose, pedagogy, or modes of accountability (Kappan, September 2013). The OECD notes that the age range birth to three years is of special concern. How to achieve that blend of care and nurture rich in early experience and appropriate learning, embedded in a real relationship with the family, vexes many policy makers. The gradual upgrading and provision of longer training of higher quality has proved almost too much for some governments, including those of England, Australia and some provinces of Canada. There are also some groups of parents and community who (for ideological reasons) actively oppose state provision of ECEC, especially for the under-threes. With increased migration across many countries have come families who do not see the need for ECEC, or, at the very least, prefer their children to be at home for as long as possible.

There is no over-riding single cause for the current state of ECEC provision in the world; rather, there is a coalescing of forces and changes that impact critically on our children. The main drivers seem to be as follows (not in any rank order):

- the slow but gradual emancipation of women;
- efficient, cheap and safe contraception;

- an overall decline in the birth rate in OECD countries;
- increasing numbers of women in the workforce and in higher education;
- high divorce rates in western societies;
- compelling research on early brain development;
- the persistent and debilitating effects of poverty and the roots of crime;
- conflicting value systems in a fluid, post-modern world;
- the powerful and universal influence of technology and the media;
- the globalisation and interlinking of economies.

The OECD (2006) records ten imperatives for policy in respect of early childhood. They are set out thus (author précis):

1 To provide a system that reduces child poverty.

2 To adopt an integrated vision of the ECEC system and organise accordingly.

3 To coordinate and steer the national system from the centre, whilst at the same time ensuring detailed local involvement.

4 To allocate adequate public funds so as to achieve quality pedagogy and care.

5 To pay special attention to the 'under-served' birth to three years age range within a thoroughly integrated vision of continuity.

6 To focus research and resources on children with diverse learning patterns and reduce targeting and remedial approaches.

7 To value and encourage family and community involvement.

8 To use the stakeholders and the professions to help co-construct broad, sustainable and appropriate programme/curriculum goals.

9 Adequately to train staff and provide continued professional development. Engage them in participatory approaches to quality practice.

10 To foster the creation of visionary, broad perspectives of learning, participation and democratic ideals.

The importance of context

Constructs, concepts, beliefs and perceptions are all ways of encapsulating ideas. No concept can exist without a context in which it is framed or occurs. An idea is partly shaped by its context and policies about what we do with our young occur within a set of beliefs, values and perceptions that help shape the policy. It is a mistake to see this as a cool, dispassionate, evidence-based affair. Policy makers are mortal creatures and their judgements are sometimes idiosyncratic, ideologically committed and highly personal. It is a brave senior civil servant who asks, 'Minister show me your evidence and sample size'.

Early childhood education and care occur within a context of ways that the culture and its communities view their children. Such views reflect beliefs and fashions of the era and sometimes more immediately local needs, too. (The use of corporal punishment in England is a good example; and there are still substantial groups of parents who think it important.) In many countries children are done unto, despite those countries being signatories to the UN Convention on the Rights of the Child. Kandel (the 'father' of comparative education) was reputed to have said that by the way a culture treated its children, so might one assess the quality of its culture. It is a sobering thought for the British, since their whole education system can be said to still display the bones of a class system and certainly a system that is utilised by the housing market! Live here and you are guaranteed companions who see education in the same light as yourself. Live there and your views may well be dissonant with the generally accepted culture of the district. Opportunities for high quality ECEC may still be an accident of location or birth, as it is for gaining access to the education system as a whole.

This chapter attempts to place ECEC in context of the big picture, dealing with certain ideas and constraints that affect the service and the training (or otherwise) of professionals who work with children. The shorthand ECEC (early childhood education and care) is used in this chapter and is pertinent for those from birth to about eight years (there are arguments about where/when early childhood ends and little convincing evidence for it being 'hard and fast'); it is a convention followed by the OECD, UNICEF and many European countries including Great Britain. Pivotal to those context lists set out earlier is a summary of some of the main implications of our more recent knowledge (the last twenty-five years, or so) on the development of the brain. Professionals, from potters to paediatricians, cannot escape the discipline of the clay they work with. The OECD's goal of well-trained professionals has to encompass a real understanding of what Bruner once called 'the entering characteristics of the learners' (ECL). Knowledge of the child and her well-being is absolutely central, as the OECD's *Starting Strong*, a study of ECEC in twenty countries, demonstrates (OECD 2001, 2006).

Influences on the curriculum for the young child

At the end of the chapter is a short summary of contextual features that appear to press in on, or facilitate, the provision of ECEC. A broadly ecological approach is employed and from time to time references will be drawn from other disciplines and from other countries. By 'ecological' I mean noting, listing and mapping those contextual features that influence the young child. The child is central to the map, or target; influences on the developing child are then mapped as highly significant, or less so. In this chapter the development of the brain is taken as the most significant feature, embedded in all we do in ECEC, yet over-riding and central to the other features identified (see Bronfenbrenner 1979).

As already stated, policy does not occur in a vacuum and the increasing bureaucratisation of education in general, as an arm of the state, is noted as itself an increasingly powerful contextual feature. Many countries have determined a 'curriculum' for even their very young and, where once in universities there were departments given to discussion and research on curriculum and philosophy, now there are few and their interventions are limited and often outside the real courts of discussion (central or state government). Australia has a process-oriented 'framework', the 'Early Years Learning Framework' (EYLF) for ECEC, approximately birth to six years. It commissioned university staff to write it (2010). Such an approach was not necessarily approved of by all the Australian states. At least two have stuck to their own public servant-derived content for ECEC. And, unlike the era of the Plowden Report (CACE 1967), it is currently (in 2014) rather difficult to see the Department for Education in England acting upon research input from universities on the best curricula for ECEC!

Advances in communication change the context, too, and mean that systems, especially apparent successes in the curriculum – literacy and maths particularly – in (say) Sweden or Finland, Australia or the USA, are quickly relayed to policy makers in other countries. The OECD has a direct concern that they should be and sees that as part of its role. Often a form of 'Chinese Whispers' occurs, such that ideas are changed somewhat in transit, or are misunderstood, or exaggerated. Moreover, very few of the ideas are that new. For instance, though there may be up-to-date research going on about the apparent connection between poor literacy rates and poverty, the connection and some of its effects, if not its subtleties, have been noted for many years.

Early education ideology

Thus, the chapter does not contain detailed descriptions of the latest research in cognitive development, or of the social psychology of policy making. Rather, it is about the shorthand constructs which are traded, used as the basis for ideological views of what is appropriate; it is about opinions and attitudes, contains 'one-liners' about how the research may be interpreted. What the chapter *does* do is attempt to set out the main contextual features and list and summarise the major constraints noted by others, such as those by the OECD, UNICEF, UNESCO, or specific governments. Most of the constructs are not discrete; they affect our views of other constructs; they may be somewhat messily tangled up with them. Fashion plays a part and perspectives are often complex and more culturally specific than some might think. Throughout it all we must remember Kandel's point, that culture is highly salient. By the way a culture regards its children and 'caters' for them, so we may register something of the quality of that culture itself. We cannot escape Mead's comment either. We look through eyes that are peculiarly our own. Such a view has a profound effect on how we see not only our policy, but the over-arching classic sociological divisions of gender and poverty themselves. Finally we should recall Chesterton's old adage, 'He who simplifies simply lies', and therefore treat the following summaries and sweeping generalisations with caution.

The child and our attitudes towards her

The child is father of the man.

William Wordsworth (1770–1850)

The importance of childhood as an important stage in life has long been recognised and documented by many authors, including Juvenal, Shakespeare, Freud and Spock. Observations by parents, teachers, paediatricians and psychologists also tell us that early experience coupled with the genetic legacy seem to build within us the highways of personality, such that the behaviour of (say) the two or three year old can be remarkably predictive and give indications of how the mature adult may well behave. A classic long-term study which underscores such prediction is the famous Dunedin study on a substantial cohort of one thousand children (see Silva and Stanton 1996). There are many others.

It was Robert Reiner, the film producer, who was attributed with the saying, 'After four your brain is cooked'. And, though this is very deterministic and tends to negate the classic re-negotiation of personality that often takes place during adolescence, it is remarkably 'pithy' and apt. What we should dwell upon is that we now have convincing evidence that there is much in it and that evidence comes directly from neuroscience and developmental psychology.

The brain and social development

It is unwise to be too deterministic and equally unwise to omit the 'hard-wired' element of human curiosity and adaptability, but we know from many studies undertaken in the last twenty-five years or so that early childhood is a period of devastating power and prediction for a human's development. It seems to hold much salience for policy makers and therefore needs awareness and careful attention. All professionals who work with children and ideally all parents, too, should know at least the bare bones of what follows about early brain development and its con-nection with social interaction during upbringing.

Early childhood, and especially that period birth to three or four years, is the time when the human organism responds to the environ-ment with such malleability that the very architecture of the brain is affected substantially. The responsiveness of even the very new-born is well documented (Shonkoff and Phillips 2000) and relationships with significant others seem to fuel the driving force behind it all. Above all, we have clear indications that the young brain thrives best in an atmosphere of love and consistency in a reliable socio-emotional environment; one best characterised as exhibiting security and high quality attachment, where others are mature enough and available emotionally to provide comfort and support when needed (Gerhardt 2004). Within this complex mix lie the rich possibilities of language and meaning, appropriate risk taking, exploration and persistence and some degree of choice. What Roberts (2010) calls 'companionable learning' may be a vital feature in all this. As many professional carers would acknowledge, interaction with others helps scaffold the thinking in the young child's questioning brain. The verbal tennis of 'why, why, why' becomes a vital avenue to knowledge.

Equally important, we know that the obverse is dangerous. Impoverished early experiences are debilitating and, if persistent, can critically limit physical and mental well-being. Crime and disconnection have their roots in the cradle and in stunted synapse connections in the infant brain. Neglect erodes relationships, inhibits learning and creates a poor 'seedbed' for sensitive growth. It casts a long misshapen shadow over that human's growth and development. The analytic couch and the longitudinal study give proof to such a view, eventually blighting adulthood and creating destructive circumstances for others within that individual's social orbit. Gerhardt (2004) refers to this as 'active harm'.

In the 1920s Mead said that all learning is social, yet, as he put it when discussing perception, we look through eyes that are peculiarly our own. One cannot be said to have much personality in a desert. One's identity, one's sense of self, depends upon, develops with, models upon and borrows from interaction with salient others. In infancy, as our brain develops and generalised perceptions form and focus and sharpen, feedback becomes ever more crucial.

Higher functioning of the brain

As early as the 1930s, Vygotsky (a psychologist with high current credibility and whose views resonate with views of social constructivism) wrote that every function in a child's development appears twice: first on the social level (inter-psychologically) and then inside the child's mind (intra-psychologically). He maintained that all higher functioning of the brain originated in actual relations between individuals (Vygotsky 1978).

The paradox is that, from a satisfying symbiosis of relationships in the early stages of infancy, and in the shadow of supportive (or otherwise) adults, grows the gradual understanding of ourselves as separate, autonomous and unique. The success of this with the initial caretakers and the burgeoning exploration which the child is permitted by the caretakers has been well documented. Children make safe 'sorties' out into the world, but are also keeping a glance to see that mother, or trusted carer, is not far away. This process depends on close attachment and safe interplay and modest risk taking. We are constructed 'brick by brick' and lack of confidence and fault lines will show permanently if substantial traumas or especially hostile conditions are experienced. We learn our value and our agency from others and the 'best' early learning is clearly that which involves our motivation (often expressed as 'engagement') and our self-esteem. The child's brain is especially receptive and constructs attributions of causality: what works, how things happen, what appears to be reliably predicted and contiguous. We learn what is held to be of value in the company of other two and three year olds and especially in the company of parents and family.

When considering the early development of the brain it is unwise to be too deterministic, but equally unwise to forget the large genetic component in its makeup.

Scientific progress

There is no doubt that magnetic resonance imaging (MRI) has made a major contribution to our knowledge of the brain and how it develops. Using it we can measure blood flow and highlight actual brain activity whilst performing tasks, resting, or undergoing a life-threatening situation. The technique is a valuable diagnostic and learning tool and has provided useful information on how the brain develops, trims and adds neuron synapse connections during adverse and optimal conditions. However, views on the importance of certain aspects of brain research and what it means are not congruent (in 2014). For instance, fifteen years ago McCain and Mustard (1999) referred to critical periods for learning in infancy: a popular idea with policy makers and parents in the decade which followed; but such windows of opportunity proved difficult to replicate and confirm or deny. There are critical periods in the development of animals other than humans, for instance that of vision in domestic kittens. It is difficult to apply these findings to children. Thus it is important to be aware of the debate and its continued controversy. Wynder stated,

> It is the consensus of the participants (Medical seminar) that a critical period exists during which the synapses of the dendrites are most ready for appropriate stimulation, be it through words, music, love, touch or caring. If these synapses are not so stimulated early, they may never develop.
>
> (1998: 166)

Bailey suggests a compromise (one with practical application and use):

> The importance of timing lies not within a set of age parameters, but rather in the match between experiences provided, the child's

developmental status, and the child's need or readiness to learn a particular skill or concept.

(2002: 294)

Brain cells are built during the foetal stage and, after birth, some trillions of connections are gradually established and put to use; those that are not appear to erode. The connections cluster and form stored cumulative experiences (constructs or 'maps') that themselves help to govern the storage, coordination, sorting and transmission of information. The constant change in the networks and their burgeoning sophistication are the direct result of contact, observation and experience, added to repetition and emotional reward. This last is partly centred upon curiosity, which seems to be 'hard-wired' into the young. Processes of 'selective amplification' occur in direct relationship to the frequency and intensity of the environmental stimulation. Furthermore, all this is embedded in attachment, consistency, recency and mimicry, such that, in practical terms, all learning is socially constructed. According to Gerhardt (2004), the first 'higher brain' capacities to develop are social and they develop in response to social experience. She suggests that rather than holding up flashcards to a baby, it would be more appropriate to the baby's stage of development to simply hold him and enjoy him.

What is clear is that neuron-synapse connections are produced in over-abundance during the early post-natal period. Those concerned with 'mapping' of social response are crucially linked to the level of interaction between the child, its parents and carers.

How children respond

This is not 'rocket science'. It has been known for a long time and is well established in literature, in folklore and in the writings of psycho-therapists and educationists. In short, the characteristic way a close adult behaves will influence the child's behaviour. This is clearly implicated in establishing individual patterns of brain development. It sets up and reinforces the common avenues of expectation that begin to typify a person's response to the environment. It underpins differently named (but similar) constructs used by developmental psychologists: e.g. attribution theory, social learning theory, locus of control, causality.

We also know some of the associated bio-chemical factors. For instance, if persistent stress occurs, either during foetal or post-natal development, the brain is likely to produce serotonin and noradrenaline at above-normal levels. Such over-activity eventually becomes 'typical' in that person, feeding back to affect both response and behaviour regulation. Both hormones are impulse regulators whose levels in the brain critically affect behaviour and the body's 'alarm system'. Stress and the production of cortisol, the stress hormone (Perry 1997; Greenspan 1997), are fairly well researched areas of concern and, whilst there are substantial individual differences, some children will respond with high cortisol production to strange or revised organisational arrangements, such as a new adult present, a new mode of working, or a change in environment (Sajaniemi *et al.* 2011).

An important thing to note is that, whilst plasticity and process are vital in brain development, variations in outcome are very large and seem to be associated with considerable differences in rates of development. It is clearly unwise to think of early learning as irredeemable, but it is equally inadvisable to pay insufficient heed to it. Countless studies show a high degree of predictability between the behaviour of (say) a three year old and that at 23. We also know that the brain continues to grow during adolescence and that learning continues throughout life. Higher order thinking protocols can be changed at any stage in life, though it is difficult to do this over a base of strongly internalised childhood learning (Gerhardt 2004).

Foundations of language

During a 'normal' childhood, especially during the first three years or so of life, the foundations of language (for which we seem at least partially 'hard-wired') are laid down securely, as are the major parameters of attitudes and dispositions towards others and the outside world. There are significant gender differences in the brain too, with the female brain somewhat smaller, but denser in grey matter. Boys and girls, women and men are often better at different things. Be careful, however, for within-group variations are considerable and the 'nature/nurture' debate cannot be resolved easily. Females have been observed as better at 'multi-tasking', at matching items at speed and at most language function. Males tend to be better at gross motor movement and mechanical and spatial skills. The point at issue here is that, while there are almost certainly a host of genetic pre-dispositions, the tasks of childhood are overlaid with cultural intent, family and social meaning and reward very early on in the child's lifetime (Smith 2001; Bailey 2002).

It seems that some children are more vulnerable to stress (Sajaniemi *et al.* 2011) and some are markedly more resilient. Some stress is necessary for normal human functioning and for facing challenge, and challenge often precedes repetition and eventual mastery. In extreme cases, where highly stressful events have become the norm at an early developmental stage, the human brain responds with a disrupted, irregular and eventually dysfunctional series of responses and these may well limit the range of reaction the child can make.

Essential conditions for learning

Advances over the last twenty years or so have led to a wide understanding of the centrality and vitality of the early years of childhood. Research certainly supports the view that the brain thrives and grows best in a nurturing social environment that provides consistency and reliability of attachment, together with interventions that secure the child yet enable her to explore safely, where a modest amount of risk yields rewards and appropriate achievement. It cannot be said, however, that research supports any specific or universal features of curriculum design or styles of learning that should be imposed on all children at a certain age. Ideological commitment does that, not research on the brain and its development. We may have rough indicators, but that is all.

According to Lally (2007), we can prepare the 'optimal conditions' for effective learning by ensuring that the child has a close and loving caregiver, such that there is consistent attachment. Continuity is important (see previous comments on cortisol and stress). See that the child has the opportunity for small groups and a chance for genuine intimacy (the creation of 'pseudo-siblings'). Ensure that care and response are always personalised, are appropriately matched and aware of special needs and of family and cultural context. Note that such conditions do not easily dictate content or specific hierarchies of learning.

We should also note that first parturition is currently at about the age of 30 in young women in the UK and that the TFR (total fertility rate) is about 1.9 children per woman. The rate has risen a little since 2000, when it was approximately 1.7 (the average for the EU is about 1.6). This means that many families across the UK and Europe have only one child, and may well have both parents in full-time employment. I have sometimes termed this the case of 'the only, lonely child' and use the term 'pseudo-siblings' to emphasise the importance of shared experience with others. The importance of ECEC is all the greater because of this factor, and social learning becomes a critical feature in the day-to-day nurture of infants. Years ago much social learning occurred within the family and its largish number of children. It is vital that the child has experience of sharing, turn-taking, awareness of others' needs and the way to relate to others. The attribution of causality seems to best grow alongside such experience (Office for National Statistics 2013).

The ecological map itself

- Most governments seem convinced ECEC is necessary, and that integration with health and social provision is important and effective, but both integration and age range (birth to eight) are compromised by many countries' existing traditions, names and categories. No really good rationale for the stage finishing at 'eight'. Terminology, such as 'preschool', 'kindergarten', 'long day care', 'nursery', is often imprecise. The under-threes are often poorly served in terms of institution, and the mixed voluntary style of provision (playgroups are a good example) is often the only relaxed, supportive access which parents and children have for each other in those first three years.

- Mixed models of financing system throughout the OECD's thirty-four countries. Mixed models of provision ... private, community, state, religious, etc. Many subsidised by payments to parent: i.e. childcare benefit, family support monies; commonly seen as a demand-side approach; many by subsidies direct to institutions (supply-side). Some suggestion that supply-side rather more equitable and efficient. Iceland (until recently) and Denmark put in the highest proportion of GDP: 1.6–1.7 per cent (see Lynch 2007). England had well over 3,000 integrated Children's Centres by 2011. Part of the then Labour government policy.

- Many governments, whether of left or right leaning, appear to be instituting curriculum outlines, target-setting and measured outcomes (testing at ages four or five years). This is the current orthodoxy. Often the claim is that parents want/need the data for an informed 'choice'. The Nordic countries tend to have very 'light touch' outlines which largely depend on the professionalism of the teachers/carers, emphasising democracy, play and individual agency and slightly separating kindergarten (age six to seven, which can take place in school *or* childcare) and ECEC (under six).

- Accreditation and 'standards'. Who 'controls and ensures' them, especially for the under-compulsory-school-age cohorts? Difficult question in large federal systems (Australia, USA and Canada, for instance). Nevertheless, a vital aspect for all countries. The licensing of institutions that provide for parents and small children can vary from country to country, from a full, sometimes bureaucratic insistence on trained staff and a curriculum framework to simple, clear safety and hygiene procedures.

- Big differences between countries in respect of professional training and community/cultural regard for staff. For this age range, staff largely female throughout the OECD. (Length and status of training very important.) Finland commonly educates its kindergarten teachers for five-plus years. There is great competition for student places.

- Broadly speaking, Nordics go for long training and relatively low interference; professional judgement still regarded as very important and trusted (see curriculum comment, above).

- English-speaking populations appear to opt for *relatively* minimal staff training ... and set standards nationally (central control with maximal interference; strong bureaucratic grip?).

- Comparison of outcomes, use of population measures. Common in Australia, Canada, UK, USA. Data-driven approaches to 'continuous improvement', exit assessments: all seem very attractive to policy makers. They appear to yield tangible results, but do they? Evidence from the US and UK suggests it may be otherwise (Kappan, October 2013). Education as an intrinsic good rarely considered; most emphasis is on future economic success.

- At the same time terms like 'delivery', 'education industry', 'quality', 'human development' and 'engagement' (i.e. fairly nebulous, often somewhat ambiguous constructs) are used a lot ... especially by politicians, economists and by health specialists (these are 'weasel words'). UNICEF unable to assess young children on such measures and had to rely on some very basic material plus self-comment for its sample of children over 12. Terms like 'well-being' and 'resilience', though useful, are usually 'situationally-specific' and temporal.

- Child abuse: no country seems quite clear about how to deal with 'lethal' parents or predatory adults and how to ensure systems that filter out disaster. Parent training, parent support both useful, but difficult to stop a parent who really wants to harm a child. Child abuse a big driver of legislation and concern (possibly out of proportion to actual incidents?).

- Partly because of the preceding point, risk and litigation are taken almost too fearfully/restrictively in English-speaking nations (American influence?). Some danger that adventure and modest risk will become untenable and diminish adventure and the quality of children's learning and enjoyment.

- No real evidence that an early start to compulsory schooling at five to seven years makes much difference, but plenty of evidence that ECEC itself makes a long-term difference. Lots of research on transition, but much rather equivocal. Still big debates about 'universality' of provision of ECEC as opposed to 'targeting' children apparently 'at risk'. Some countries consider making kindergarten compulsory. Some dangers of 'schoolification' of ECEC and play not fully understood as iconic, appropriate and vital for early learning (UNESCO 2002).

- Limited views of national curricula and centrally mandated frameworks. Some evidence that British national curriculum has been motivationally disastrous since 1988. Teaching profession very sceptical in UK. Furthermore, even earlier, there was no real evidence that Plowden's (CACE 1967) so-called 'child-centred' approaches had failed previously. Paradox in that Reggio Emilia (Italy) is now extolled almost universally, yet is a very child-centred, project-based, often child-'choice' approach.

- Nevertheless, some strident views that 'standards', especially those of literacy in the age range five to eight, have fallen over the years. (US especially ... major focus in policy of 'No Child Left Behind' (NCLB).) Literacy is a central concern in England and official views of synthetic phonics are very much to the fore. There is considerable evidence that literacy and enjoyment of reading go hand in hand with emotional security, parental interest and so on in UK (Sylva *et al.* 2004).

- Evidence everywhere showing girls seem to do better at all stages of education.

- Overwhelming evidence that major personality traits and cognitive styles and dispositions laid down in the first three or four years of life. (Are we born with certain 'pre-dispositions' and are appropriate dispositions and attitudes the prime goals of any ECEC curricular framework?)

- Evidence that boys are some five to six times more likely to be 'behind' the girls in certain basic skills, such as reading.

- Evidence that large portions of childhood are spent watching TV/using IT. Concomitant evidence of less time spent with parents. Some worry therefore about interactive quality of communication.

- Considerable evidence that violence portrayed in media is counter-productive and damaging for society. (Also some concerns about the possible over-sexualisation of young girls?)

- Some evidence that, in reality, ECEC provides a 'family experience' and the company of 'pseudo-siblings'.

- Ratios matter with very young. One adult to four children now fairly common in EU under age two.

- Overwhelming evidence internationally that quality of service depends primarily on quality of professional training and good leadership.

Postscript

Lastly, in the big ecological picture, what might one envisage as the best experience for every child born into the twenty-first century?

> To be born into a friendly, sensitive environment, which is able to bathe the child in good healthy practices: good food, language, love and a sense of belonging.
> To be born into a safe place where there is no fear, other than the low level risk of trying.
> To be born into a world replete with interesting sensations, of other adults and children.
> To be born into a world where possibilities are exciting and endless.
> To be born into a world where moral principles are commonly seen and exemplified in everyday life.
>
> (Gammage 2008)

References

Bailey, D.B. (2002) Are critical periods critical for early childhood education? The role of timing in early childhood pedagogy. *Early Childhood Research Quarterly* 17: 281–294.

Bronfenbrenner, U. (1979) *The Ecology of Human Development: Experiments in Nature and Design.* Cambridge, MA: Harvard University Press.

Central Advisory Council for Education (CACE) (1967) *Children and Their Primary Schools* (Plowden Report), vol. 1. London: HMSO.

Gammage, P. (2008) Early childhood education and care: the social agenda. Online Outreach paper no. 4. www.bernardvanleer.org

Gerhardt, S. (2004) *Why Love Matters: How Affection Shapes a Baby's Brain.* London: Routledge.

Greenspan, S. (1997) *The Growth of the Mind.* New York: Addison-Wesley.

Kappan (September 2013) Which way do we go? *Phi Delta Kappan.*

Kappan (October 2013) Teaching and learning the skills needed for academic success. *Phi Delta Kappan.*

Lally, R. (2007) The developing child and the curriculum. Seminar on 'Our Children the Future', 21 September, Adelaide, South Australia.

Lynch, R. (2007) *Enriching Children, Enriching the Nation.* Chicago: Foundation for Child Development.

McCain, M.N. and Mustard, J.F. (1999) Reversing the real brain drain, early years study: Final Report. Toronto.

OECD (2001) *Starting Strong: Early Childhood Education and Care 1.* Paris: Organisation for Economic Cooperation and Development.

OECD (2006) *Starting Strong: Early Childhood Education and Care 2.* Paris: Organisation for Economic Cooperation and Development.

Office for National Statistics (2013) Why has the fertility rate risen over the last decade in England and Wales? Part of Birth Summary Tables – England and Wales, 2011 (final release 17 June 2013).

Perry, B. (1997) How children are affected by traumatic experiences. *Breakthrough Medicine.* Talk given on Radio Houston, 17 September 1997. Available in collection of articles at http:// teacher.scho;astic.com/

Roberts, R. (2010) *Wellbeing from Birth.* London: Sage.

Sajaniemi, N. *et al.* (2011) Children's cortisol patterns and the quality of the early learning environment. *European Early Childhood Research Journal,* 19, 1: 45–62.

Shonkoff, J. and Phillips, D. (2000) *From Neurons to Neighborhoods: The Science of Early Child Development*. Washington, DC: National Academic Press.

Silva, P.A. and Stanton, W.R. (eds) (1996) *From Child to Adult: The Dunedin Multidisciplinary Health and Development Study*. Oxford: Oxford University Press.

Smith, A. (2001) *The Brain's Behind It*. London: Network Educational Press.

Sylva, K. *et al.* (2004) *The Effective Provision of Pre-School Education: The Final Report*. London: Department for Education and Skills, Sure Start Publications and Institute of Education.

UNESCO (2002) *Integrating Early Childhood into Education: The Case of Sweden*. Policy Brief on Early Childhood, May, Washington, DC: United Nations Educational, Scientific and Cultural Organisation.

Vygotsky, L.S. (1978) *Mind in Society: The Development of Higher Psychological Processes*. Cambridge, MA: Harvard University Press.

Wynder, E. (1998) Introduction to report on the conference on 'The Critical Period of Brain Development', *Preventive Medicine*, 27: 166–167.

Early childhood environments

Long-term consequences of early childhood education and parenting

Edward Melhuish

Introduction

In a changing world the skills that children need to acquire in order to have good life chances are increasing and becoming more complex. However there are great differences in the health and development of individuals linked to their social origins. Every parent and professional working with children has a view on how children thrive drawn from their experience and anecdotal stories. However there is now evidence from longitudinal and other research that should guide both policy and practice. Children from poor families are less likely to be successful in school and are more likely to have poorer health and to engage in crime and other problem behaviour later in life (Holzer *et al.* 2007). The stress that can come from poverty can shape a child's neuro-biology, leading directly to poorer outcomes in adulthood (Shonkoff and Phillips 2000). In order to improve these circumstances, social exclusion, educational reform and public health policies need to be integrated. However, despite several decades of social, educational and public health reform, the impact of social origins on child outcomes persists and is even increasing. This results in an enormous waste of the talents of those individuals who grow up in disadvantaged circumstances, as their potential contribution to society is never fully realised. Additionally there is an extra load on society as these individuals who mature into disadvantaged youths and adults will show greater need for state resources throughout their lives, as their ability to thrive is often compromised. Thus there is both a moral dilemma – how to reduce inequality and make people's lives more fulfilled – and a social and economic dilemma in that a society with a high proportion of disadvantaged individuals, and poorer level of skills throughout the population, is less able to adapt to a world demanding higher levels of productivity to maintain living standards. These problems are exacerbated over time, as increasingly technologically advanced societies need more and newer skills from the workforce. Hence there is an increasing need for more adaptable and technically skilled populations. The aims of equality and future productivity can merge in policy through realising that learning capabilities are shaped during the first years of childhood. Thus improving life chances in early childhood can serve both the goals of reducing inequality and raising the productive capacity of a society, and research tells us that such a strategy can work.

Why should we focus on the early years? One reason is the accumulation of evidence that the child's experience in the early years has profound consequences for later life. There are many studies presenting a consistent picture that adversity in early life, such as frequently accompanies child poverty, is linked to poor adult mental and physical health, adult mortality, anti-social and criminal behaviour, substance abuse, and poor literacy and academic achievement. Heckman (2006) considers data derived from several different studies, usually with disadvantaged groups of children, and has shown that the return on investment is much higher in the preschool years than in the school years, which is higher than for the post-school years; i.e. investment in the early years makes sound economic sense.

The evidence

In making conclusions from the evidence on early childhood education and care (ECEC), we need to distinguish between results for 0–3 years, where the research evidence is mixed, with some studies indicating benefits, some indicating negative effects and some studies indicating no effects at all. The discrepant results for studies of childcare for children 0–3 years probably reflects different effects for different populations, different ages, different types of children, as well as differing qualities of childcare for differing settings and differing populations. When studies of ECEC for children over three years are considered, the evidence of benefits for children is clear and there are almost universal benefits for children associated with the various forms of group-based ECEC attended by children from 3 years upwards. Also the benefits increase the greater the quality of the preschool provision, defined in terms of how well the centres serve children's developmental needs (Melhuish 2004).

The provision of ECEC for children aged 3 years and older has been explored in a number of studies. One study focusing on the general population that has been influential in this area is the Effective Pre-school, Primary and Secondary Education (EPPSE) Project. EPPSE has addressed the question of the longer-term impact of ECEC for children who were young at a time when there was no universal provision of ECEC in the UK. This study focused on early childhood education in all types of preschool centre that existed in England at the time of the study. These centres all included children around 3 years of age and older, but some centres also included younger children. This longitudinal study of 3,000 children has also studied the effects of various child, family and home characteristics upon child development. The results from EPPSE up to ages 11 and 14 are summarised in Sylva *et al.* (2010, 2012).

Children whose first language was not English, who had low birth-weight, or who had three or more siblings all did worse on cognitive development. Girls did better than boys. Parent education and social class were also important influences upon child development, and children from poor families did worse. However the strongest effect of all, when children started school, was for the home learning environment, a measure of learning opportunities in the home. Where the child had more frequent opportunities for learning activities in the home, the child did better on all aspects of child development. These effects at the start of school were after taking account of all other child, parent and home characteristics, and the results can be summarised as '*What parents do is more important than who parents are*' (Melhuish *et al.* 2001). This reflects the start-of-school finding that the home learning environment had an equal or more powerful effect upon child development than parents' education or social class.

After allowing for all these background factor effects, the question of whether attending a preschool centre mattered was considered. The project established not only whether preschool overall had an effect but

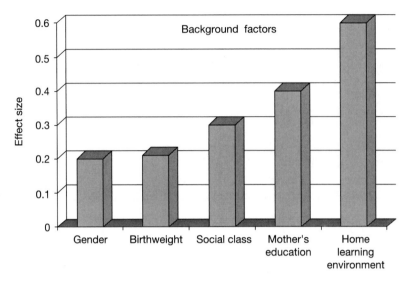

Figure 2.1 Child and family factors and early literacy at start of school

The effect sizes are in standard deviation units to facilitate comparisons.

also which preschool centres were having a greater or lesser effect than others. The main effects, upon literacy, associated with different child, family and home characteristics (Sammons *et al.* 2002) are shown in Figure 2.1.

In addition the effects of preschool were evident at the start of primary school. On measures of language, literacy and numeracy the preschool group did better. On average the benefit of preschool was 0.2 of a standard deviation above that of the no-preschool group. As well as measuring the effect of preschool overall, there were data on the quality of the preschool environments from direct observation, and also on the amount of time that the child had attended preschool. We found that both quality and duration of preschool were important. Where children had been to preschool for a longer duration, benefits were greater. Also the effects varied by quality of ECEC, with higher quality producing greater benefits (Sammons *et al.* 2002; Sylva *et al.* 2004). There were similar benefits for social development.

ECEC effects for primary school attainment

After the children had been at school for two years we collected more information on their development. The benefits of preschool, particularly higher quality preschool, were still apparent. When children have been

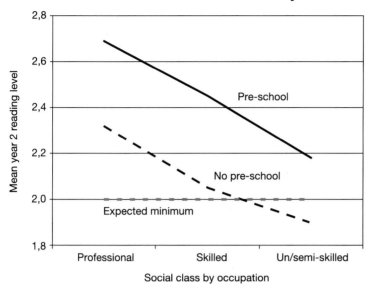

Figure 2.2 Key Stage 2 reading by preschool attendance and social class

in school for three years all children in England take national assessments in reading, mathematics and science. We used this data to see if the effects of preschool persisted. The results are illustrated in graph form in Figure 2.2.

For all social class groups the effect of preschool was clear, and similar for all groups. However there is a minimum acceptable level of attainment for all children (level 2). While all social class groups who received preschool education had scored, on average, above the minimum level, in the disadvantaged group (unskilled or unemployed) children scored, on average, below the minimum acceptable level of attainment if they had not had preschool education. This indicates that the consequences of not having preschool education are particularly important for disadvantaged children.

What makes ECEC effective?

The Effective Provision of Pre-School Education (EPPE) study was able to identify the most effective preschools that produced the most developmental benefit for children. We undertook qualitative case studies of the most effective and average preschools to investigate what processes were associated with particularly effective preschools. In these case studies (Siraj-Blatchford *et al.* 2003, 2005) the researchers did not know which preschools had been identified as effective or ineffective, so their observations were not biased. These case studies identified five areas that were particularly important:

1 Quality of adult–child verbal interaction.

2 Staff knowledge and understanding of the curriculum.

3 Staff knowledge of how children learn.

4 Adult skills in helping children resolve conflicts.

5 Helping parents to support children's learning at home.

Combining the effects of school

In order to continue to investigate children's development later, it was important to be able to take account of the effects of the school upon the children in the study. Therefore a measure of the effectiveness of schools was devised.

In England all children take national assessments in reading, mathematics and science at ages 7 and 11. Analyses considered the child's progress from age 7 to age 11 in English, mathematics and science as a function of the child and area characteristics. It was possible to measure the effectiveness of each primary school in England. For some schools children did better than expected – effective schools – and for some schools children did worse than expected – ineffective schools. Also the effectiveness of a school could be analysed for children of different levels of ability. We found that being in an effective school had a bigger influence on low ability pupils than on high ability pupils.

What affects child outcomes?

We could analyse children's development in terms of child, family, home learning environment, preschool and school factors (see Figure 2.3).

The graph in Figure 2.4 (Melhuish 2011; Sammons et al. 2008) shows the relative size of effects (standard deviation units) of a range of variables upon children's achievement in literacy and numeracy, as measured by national assessments, at age 11.

Mother's education and the home learning environment (measured at age 3–4) are the strongest influences upon children's attainment.

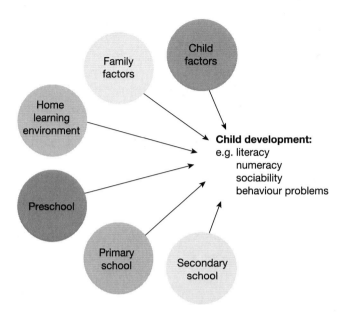

Figure 2.3 Modelling later outcomes

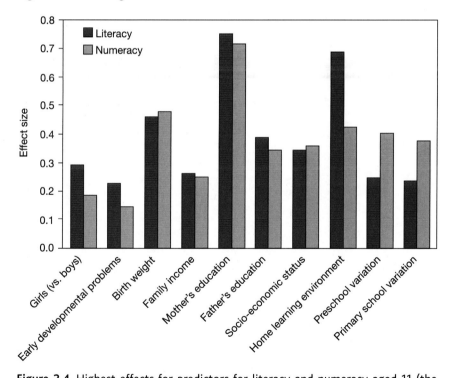

Figure 2.4 Highest effects for predictors for literacy and numeracy aged 11 (the effect sizes are in standard deviation units to facilitate comparison between predictors)

However preschool effectiveness and primary school effectiveness are also important influences and are very similar in their importance, and account for about half as much variance as home factors. While the effects displayed are for attainment in literacy and numeracy, there are also substantial similar effects upon children's social development.

In summary we can conclude that there are three key elements of a child's environment for educational success:

1 Good home learning environment.

2 Good preschools.

3 Good primary schools.

Other things being equal, those children with all three will outperform children with two, who will outperform children with one, who will outperform children with none.

Conclusions from EPPSE:

1 From age 2 all children will benefit from preschool education.

2 The quality of preschool matters.

3 The duration of preschool matters in the early school years.

4 Part-time preschool has equal benefit to full-time.

5 For medium and high quality preschool, benefits persist.

Sure Start

In the UK a major change in early years services was the government initiative called Sure Start. In 1998 a UK government review (HM Treasury 1998) concluded that disadvantage among young children was increasing and early intervention could alleviate poor outcomes. It proposed that early years programmes should involve all relevant bodies, and be *area-based*, with *all* children under four and their families in an area as clients. This approach tried to avoid the stigmatisation associated with services for disadvantaged families while simultaneously fostering community development and child and family functioning. In July 1998, the then Chancellor of the Exchequer, Gordon Brown, announced the Sure Start initiative which was to focus on the 20 per cent most deprived areas, which included around 51 per cent of children in families with incomes 60 per cent or less than the national median (official poverty line) (Melhuish and Hall 2007).

Sure Start programmes started in 2000. A typical programme included 800 preschool children, and 250 Sure Start programmes were planned to start by 2002, to support 187,000 children, 18 per cent of poor preschool children in England. Community control was exercised through local partnership boards comprised of local stakeholders, including health, social services, education, private and voluntary sectors, and parents. Until 2006 funding came directly from central government. While evidence from programmes with clear detailed protocols was used to justify Sure Start (e.g. Schweinhart *et al.* 1993; Ramey *et al.* 2000), Sure Start did not have a prescribed 'protocol'. All programmes were expected to provide: (1) outreach and home visiting; (2) support for families and parents; (3) support for good quality play, learning and childcare experiences for children; (4) primary and community health care and advice about child health and development and family health; and (5) support for people with special needs, but without specific guidance as to how.

The speed and amount of funding was often overwhelming in a sector previously starved of support. Only 6 per cent of the 1999 allocation was spent in that year. Despite this slow start, and without any information on the success of the initiative, the Treasury expanded Sure Start from 250 programmes in 2002 to over 500 by 2004. Thus Sure Start became a cornerstone of the campaign to reduce child poverty.

National Evaluation of Sure Start (NESS)

This evaluation started in 2001, and from the outset diversity posed challenges in that there were not several hundred programmes delivering one intervention, but several hundred unique interventions. Government decisions ruled out a randomised control trial, hence a quasi-experimental design with consequent limitations was used to compare Sure Start populations with equivalent populations not residing in Sure Start areas. The early evaluation work up to 2005 has been summarised (Belsky *et al.* 2007), with detailed reports of all the work up to 2012 available at www.ness.bbk.ac.uk.

Communities and change

Sure Start was based on the premise that the programme could affect children and families directly, and indirectly, via community changes engendered by the programme. Community characteristics were tracked over five years (Barnes 2007). Sure Start areas became home to more young children, while households dependent on benefits decreased markedly. Some aspects of crime and disorder also improved, with less burglary, school exclusions and unauthorised school absences. Moreover, children from 11 upwards demonstrated improved academic achievement. Reductions in emergency hospitalisations of children (0 to 3) for severe injury and for lower respiratory infection suggested improved health care. Also the percentage of children identified with special educational needs or eligible for disability benefits increased over 2000–2005, suggesting improved health screening. Thus there appeared to be some community improvements.

Early effects on children/families
A cross-sectional study of children and families in Sure Start and non-Sure Start areas provided mixed findings (NESS 2005). There were some overall Sure Start effects, but most effects varied by subgroup. Specifically, three year olds of non-teen mothers (86 per cent of sample) in Sure Start communities had fewer behaviour problems and greater social competence as compared with those in comparison communities, and these effects for children appeared to be mediated by Sure Start effects of less negative parenting for non-teen mothers. Adverse effects emerged, however, for children of teen mothers (14 per cent of sample) in Sure Start areas in terms of lower verbal ability and social competence and higher behaviour problems. Also children from workless households (40 per cent of sample) and from lone-parent families (33 per cent of sample) in Sure Start areas scored lower on verbal ability than equivalent children in comparison communities.

Variability in programme effectiveness
Estimates of each programme's effectiveness for outcomes were assessed, and NESS looked at why some programmes might have been more effective than others. Qualitative and quantitative data on 150 programmes was used to rate each Sure Start Local Programme on eighteen dimensions of implementation (Anning and Ball 2007). Programmes rated high on one dimension tended to score high on others, and better implemented programmes appeared to yield greater benefits (Melhuish et al. 2007).

Changes to programmes

As early findings indicated that Sure Start programmes were not having the impact hoped for, and evidence from the EPPSE project showed that integrated Children's Centres were particularly beneficial to children's development, the government decided to transform Sure Start programmes into Children's Centres. An Act of Parliament transferred control of the Sure Start Children's Centres to local authorities, which ensured that Sure Start Children's Centres became embedded within the welfare state by statute, making it difficult for any future government to eradicate Sure Start. Thus from 2006 Sure Start had more clearly specified services and guidelines, and was controlled by local government rather than central government.

Later results

In a longitudinal study, randomly-selected nine month olds seen earlier were followed up at ages three, five and seven years. Comparing children and families in Sure Start areas with those in similar non-Sure Start areas revealed beneficial effects for Sure Start areas when children were three years old on seven out of fourteen outcomes (Melhuish *et al.* 2008a). Sure Start children showed better social development, exhibiting more positive social behaviour and greater self-regulation. This result appeared to be partially a consequence of parents in Sure Start areas manifesting less negative parenting, as well as offering a more stimulating home learning environment.

When children were five years old there were improvements primarily for parenting and child health, in terms of lower rates of overweight children and better general health. For parents there was less home chaos, better home learning environments, mothers reporting greater life satisfaction and a reduction in worklessness compared to the similar families without Sure Start (NESS 2010). Similar results for parenting were also found when the children were seven years old (NESS 2012).

The disappointing finding of the Sure Start evaluation was that early improvements in child outcomes were not maintained. This appeared to be due, at least partly, to the Sure Start programmes not providing a high enough level of quality of ECEC, because when children in Sure Start areas did receive higher quality ECEC there was higher language development (Melhuish *et al.* 2010a). Thus it appeared that Sure Start needed to improve the implementation of services in order to produce the desired results. In particular the variation of results across the many

Sure Start programmes indicates that inter-agency collaboration, particularly between health and education, and the provision of high quality services can have an impact on parent outcomes and potentially child outcomes. These points are particularly relevant to interventions going to scale and serving substantial populations. Currently there is great scope for improvement in inter-agency collaboration, and the quality of services.

The future of Sure Start Children's Centres

Sure Start has been evolving and ongoing research has partly influenced this process. Later developments have clarified guidelines and service delivery. It is plausible that the improved results in the evaluation of Sure Start reflect actual changes in the impact of the programmes resulting from the increasing quality of services, greater attention to the hard-to-reach, the move to Children's Centres, as well as greater exposure to services. The results are modest but suggest that the value of Sure Start programmes had improved, at least up to 2010. The identification of the factors associated with more effective programmes informed the later improvements in Sure Start and may be part of the reason for the beneficial outcomes for children and families later found for Sure Start.

Subsequent economic recession and government changes mean the future of Sure Start is changing and unclear. As a result of spending reductions the government funding available for Sure Start services has been steadily reducing:

2010/11	£2,483m
2011/12	£2,223m
2012/13	£2,074m
2013/14	£1,709m
2014/15	£1,600m

Despite these cuts many local authorities are committed to maintain Sure Start services, as they recognise their value in supporting families and young children. The response to the new fiscal environment is revealed in the Children's Centre Census (4Children 2012) which showed that in 2011/12, centres were:

- focusing on early intervention and parenting – mirroring government priorities;

- often reducing universal sessions including stay and play and baby massage; this reflected the change in emphasis to reaching more disadvantaged parents;

- increasingly managed in 'clusters' of a number of centres; this is reflected in a revised Ofsted inspection framework that inspects such centres as a group;

- resisting introducing charges for the majority of services;

- modifying their childcare offer, often reducing full-time childcare places and some withdrawing from childcare provision altogether;

- increasing the use of volunteers; ECCE (2012) found that 18 per cent of staff in early established centres were volunteers.

The All Party Parliamentary Group for Sure Start (2013) calls for the following:

1 Coordination with health services, with health visitors, midwives and Children's Centres based together 'under one roof', for families before and after birth.

2 Children's Centres might act as childminder agencies.

3 Greater focus on supporting families from pregnancy until children are two.

4 Children's Centres will be crucial for eligible parents to take up the offer of fifteen hours of free childcare when their child is two years old (bottom 40 per cent).

5 Whitehall Departments should stop operating in silos; and see that joined up working saves money, and has the side effect of encouraging data sharing which is key to supporting new families, but often is not happening.

6 Registration of births should also take place in Children's Centres with health services and Children's Centres sharing data on births.

The All Party Parliamentary Group also noted the disengagement of Children's Centres from directly providing childcare or early education, and this change has increasingly put more of a load on nurseries and other preschool facilities.

Edward Melhuish

Policy and evidence

Countries vary enormously in their provision of early years services. Almost every developed country has set up some form of ECEC for children below school age. The differences lie in the organisational forms, the level of state subsidy, the responsible authorities and the age at which children access provision. In many countries public authorities offer subsidised places from a very early age, often from the end of statutory maternity leave. Yet, even in developed countries, the ECEC provided is often of poor or modest quality, because it is not structured to provide the best environment for nurturing children's development and well-being. The evidence indicates that ECEC must be of adequate quality to produce benefits for children.

An ideal system would involve high quality, affordable and accessible ECEC that is sufficiently flexible for either parent to return to work. The Nordic countries tend to have the best systems that combine all these features. Some wealthy countries, such as the UK, have greatly improved their systems in the last decade, but still have some way to catch up, with still much poor quality ECEC. Poorer countries vary in their provision, and also vary in their attitudes to non-family care for very young children. Nonetheless, evidence suggests that post two years of age, spending some time each week in group care that is stimulating and high quality benefits all children, and helps to ensure that children from poorer backgrounds gain more. It also is a major poverty reduction strategy, enabling parental employment and so increasing family income. Ideal provision includes multiple uses for childcare centres, including advice and support on parenting, health and diet, and wider community use, as should occur in the UK's Children's Centres, but often does not through inadequate implementation.

There remains the need to extend coverage of ECEC provision in many countries. But the quality of ECEC must also be high. European states have in recent years stated a wish to cooperate more closely at European Union (EU) level to increase the quality of ECEC. In 2006, EU ministers stated that ECEC could bring high rates of return over the life cycle, especially for the disadvantaged. In 2008 they agreed priorities for EU cooperation including how to ensure accessible, high quality preschool provision, and in 2009 they adopted a strategic framework for cooperation until 2020, which included the priority to promote generalised equitable access and reinforce the quality of the provision and teacher support in pre-primary education (European Commission 2011).

The assumption behind much policy in the last fifty years in the developed world has been that equalising educational opportunity would eliminate the effect of poverty on educational and occupational success, with no need to alter the income distribution. Research on inter-generational mobility indicates that this has been overly optimistic. In the US, the UK and France the association between parental income and their children's income (as adults) is exceptionally strong, especially in comparison to the Nordic countries. Research shows that social inheritance effects are substantially weaker in Nordic countries than in other developed countries. Esping-Andersen (2004) suggests that the key to Nordic countries' success in breaking the link between parental attainment and children's outcomes may be the provision of universal and high quality ECEC. He notes that the period when inequality in children's cognitive attainment decreased roughly corresponds to the period when universal ECEC was put in place. Experience in Finland suggests that polarisation of child outcomes can be minimised even when the average performance is very high.

In addition to the evidence from EPPSE, several other studies document the benefits of ECEC for school readiness (Gormley *et al.* 2008; Magnuson *et al.* 2004), which is greater if preschool started between two and three years of age (Loeb *et al.* 2007; Sammons *et al.* 2002). A meta-analysis of 125 early childhood education studies in the USA (Camilli *et al.* 2010) found that early childhood education was associated with substantial effects for both cognitive and socio-emotional outcomes. Preschool programmes with an emphasis on educational experiences directly delivered to the child appeared to have more impact.

Also the effects associated with ECEC are long-term; for example, preschool was associated with increased qualifications, employment, and earnings up to age 33 (Goodman and Sianesi 2005). In France *école maternelle* is a universal, free education programme with access from age three. During the 1960s and 1970s large-scale expansion led to the enrolment of three year olds increasing from 35 per cent to 90 per cent and of four year olds from 60 per cent to 100 per cent. National data reveal sizeable and persistent effects, with *école maternelle* helping children succeed in school and obtain higher wages in the labour market. Early childhood education also reduced socioeconomic inequalities as children from less advantaged backgrounds benefited more than the more advantaged (Dumas and Lefranc 2010). Likewise in Switzerland the impact of preschool expansion was associated with improved inter-generational educational mobility, with children from disadvantaged backgrounds benefiting most (Bauer and Riphahn 2009). Further evidence comes from the expansion of early childhood education in Norway, where differential implementation of preschool by municipalities revealed that preschool was associated with strong benefits for later educational and labour market outcomes (Havnes and Mogstad 2011).

Similar evidence exists outside the industrialised countries. Early childhood education has been shown to boost primary school achievement in Bangladesh (Aboud 2006), with similar results being reported for ten other countries (Montie *et al.* 2006). Examination of expansion of early childhood education in Uruguay and Argentina has also revealed clear benefits from preschool in terms of improved educational attainment (Berlinski *et al.* 2008; Berlinski *et al.* 2009).

The benefits associated with high quality ECEC are wide-ranging, covering cognitive, educational and social development. This is because different aspects of a child's development are inter-related, with development in one area helping development in another. It is difficult to say precisely what the relative size of effects is in different areas because of the problem of the relative precision of measurement for different aspects of development. However the evidence shows that just providing any ECEC is not enough. Studies from the USA (Vandell *et al.* 2010), England (Melhuish *et al.* 2008b; Sylva *et al.* 2010), Northern Ireland (Melhuish *et al.* 2010b) and Denmark (Bauchmüller *et al.* 2011) indicate that the quality of ECEC is critical for longer-term beneficial effects. The Organisation for Economic Cooperation and Development (OECD) examined educational attainment data for sixty-five countries, finding that literacy at age 15 was strongly associated with preschool participation in countries where a large proportion of the population use preschool, where it is used for more months, and where there were measures to maintain its quality. They concluded that widening access to ECEC can improve performance and equity by reducing socioeconomic disparities, if extending coverage did not compromise quality (OECD 2011).

The importance of the quality of ECEC exemplifies the critical role of implementation in service provision, whether in the private, voluntary or public sector. For example, it is of little help having a hospital that cannot provide effective medical treatment. Similarly a children's centre that does not provide children with experiences that foster their development is useless. Hence the key to the provision of high quality ECEC is the structuring of the environment to optimise the experiences of children in terms of fostering development.

Research has shown that the home learning environment is equally, if not more, important in helping children develop. Where children are provided with a range of learning opportunities in the home, their cognitive, language and social development are all improved (Melhuish *et al.* 2008c). In fact the home learning environment can have up to twice the size of effect of ECEC. However, in a democratic society it is difficult to legislate for parenting, but relatively straightforward to legislate for the provision of ECEC. One factor that differentiates more effective ECEC is staff providing parents with help with home experiences that can promote children's learning (Siraj-Blatchford *et al.* 2003). The peer group learning that occurs between parents who meet at their children's ECEC centre can also help parents in developing their knowledge and parenting skills. To some extent good quality ECEC can compensate for inadequacies in the child's home learning environment. However, a child will show the best outcomes when the home learning environment and ECEC are both supportive of the child's development. This indicates the importance of ECEC staff including parents as partners in providing the child's early experiences, and encouraging the participation of parents.

References

4Children (2012) *Sure Start Children's Centres Census 2012.*

Aboud, F.E. (2006) Evaluation of an early childhood pre-school in rural Bangladesh. *Early Childhood Research Quarterly*, 21, 46–60.

All Party Parliamentary Group for Sure Start (2013) *All Party Parliamentary Sure Start Group Report: The Way Forward for Children's Centres.* London: 4Children. www.4children.org.uk/Files/cffc42fe-49eb-43e2-b330-a1fd00b8077b/Best-Practice-for-a-Sure-Start.pdf

Anning A. and Ball, M. (2007) *Improving Services for Young Children: From Sure Start to Children's Centres.* London: Sage.

Barnes, J. (2007) How Sure Start Local Programmes areas changed. In J. Belsky, J. Barnes and E. Melhuish (eds) *The National Evaluation of Sure Start: Does Area-Based Early Intervention Work?* Bristol: Policy Press, pp. 173–194.

Bauchmüller, R., Gørtz, M. and Rasmussen, A.W. (2011) Long-run benefits from universal high-quality pre-schooling. AKF Working Paper, 2011(2), AKF. www.cser.dk/fileadmin/www.cser.dk/wp_008_rbmgawr.pdf

Bauer, P.C. and Riphahn, R.T. (2009) Age at school entry and intergenerational educational mobility. *Economics Letters*, 103, 87–90.

Belsky, J., Barnes, J. and Melhuish, E. (eds) (2007) *The National Evaluation of Sure Start: Does Area-Based Early Intervention Work?* Bristol: Policy Press.

Berlinski, S., Galiani, S. and Manacorda, M. (2008) Giving children a better start: preschool attendance and school-age profiles. *Journal of Public Economics*, 92, 1416–1440.

Berlinski, S., Galiani, S. and Gertler, P. (2009) The effect of pre-primary education on primary school performance. *Journal of Public Economics*, 93, 219–234.

Camilli, G., Vargas, S., Ryan, S. and Barnett, W.S. (2010) Meta-analysis of the effects of early education interventions on cognitive and social development. *Teachers College Record*, 112, 579–620.

Dumas, C. and Lefranc, A. (2010) Early schooling and later outcomes: evidence from preschool extension in France. Thema Working Paper no. 2010-07 (Université de Cergy Pontoise, France). http://thema.u-cergy.fr/IMG/documents/2010-07.pdf

Esping-Andersen, G. (2004) Untying the Gordian Knot of social inheritance. *Research in Social Stratification and Mobility*, 21, 115–139.

European Commission (2011) *Early Childhood Education and Care: Providing all our children with the best start for the world of tomorrow.* Brussels, COM(2011) 66 final. http://eur-lex.europa.eu/LexUriServ/LexUriServ.do?uri=COM:2011:0066:FIN:EN:PDF

Evaluation of Children's Centres in England (ECCE) (2012) *Strand 1: First Survey of Children's Centre Leaders in the Most Deprived Areas.* London: DfE.

Goodman, A. and Sianesi, B. (2005) Early education and children's outcomes: how long do the impacts last? *Fiscal Studies*, 26, 513–548.

Gormley, W., Phillips, D. and Gayer, T. (2008) Preschool programs can boost school readiness. *Science*, 320, 1723–1724.

Havnes, T. and Mogstad, M. (2011) No Child Left Behind: subsidized child care and children's long-run outcomes. *American Economic Journal: Economic Policy*, 3, 97–129.

Heckman, J.J. (2006) Skill formation and the economics of investing in disadvantaged children. *Science*, 132, 1900–1902.

HM Treasury (1998) *Comprehensive Spending Review: Cross Departmental Review of Provision for Young Children.* London: HMSO.

Holzer, H., Schanzenbach, D., Duncan, G. and Ludwig, J. (2007) The economic costs of poverty in the United States: subsequent effects of children growing up poor. Institute for Research on Poverty

Discussion Paper no. 1327-07. www.irp.wisc.edu/publications/dps/pdfs/dp132707.pdf

Loeb, S., Bridges, M., Bassok, D., Fuller, B. and Rumberger, R.W. (2007) How much is too much? The influence of pre-school centers on children's social and cognitive development. *Economics of Education Review*, 26, 52–66.

Magnuson, K., Meyers, M., Ruhm, C. and Waldfogel, J. (2004) Inequality in preschool education and school readiness. *American Educational Research Journal*, 41, 115–157.

Melhuish, E.C. (2004) *A literature review of the impact of early years provision upon young children, with emphasis given to children from disadvantaged backgrounds: Report to the Comptroller and Auditor General.* London: National Audit Office. www.nao.org.uk/publications/0304/early_years_progress.aspx

Melhuish, E.C. (2011) Preschool matters. *Science*, 333, 299–300.

Melhuish, E. and Hall, D. (2007) The policy background to Sure Start. In J. Belsky, J. Barnes and E. Melhuish (eds) *The National Evaluation of Sure Start: Does Area-Based Early Intervention Work?* Bristol: Policy Press, pp. 3–21.

Melhuish, E.C., Sylva, K., Sammons, P., Siraj-Blatchford, I. and Taggart, B. (2001) *The Effective Provision of Pre-school Education Project, Technical Paper 7: Social/behavioural and cognitive development at 3–4 years in relation to family background.* London: Institute of Education/DfES.

Melhuish, E., Belsky, J., Anning, A. *et al.* (2007) Variation in community intervention programmes and consequences for children and families: the example of Sure Start Local Programmes. *Journal of Child Psychology and Psychiatry*, 48, 543–551.

Melhuish, E., Belsky, J., Leyland, A.H., Barnes, J. and NESS Research Team *et al.* (2008a) A quasi-experimental study of effects of fully-established Sure Start Local Programmes on 3-year-old children and their families. *Lancet*, 372, 1641–1647.

Melhuish, E.C., Sylva, K., Sammons, P., Siraj-Blatchford, I., Taggart, B., Phan, M. and Malin, A. (2008b) Preschool influences on mathematics achievement. *Science*, 321, 1161–1162.

Melhuish, E.C., Sylva, K., Sammons, P., Siraj-Blatchford, I., Taggart, B. and Phan, M. (2008c) Effects of the home learning environment and preschool center experience upon literacy and numeracy development in early primary school. *Journal of Social Issues*, 64, 95–114.

Melhuish, E., Belsky, J., MacPherson, K. and Cullis, A. (2010a) The quality of group childcare settings used by 3–4 year old children in Sure Start local programme areas and the relationship with child outcomes. Research Report DFE-RR068. London: DfE.

Melhuish, E., Quinn, L., Sylva, K., Sammons, P., Siraj-Blatchford, I. and Taggart, B. (2010b) *Pre-school Experience and Key Stage 2 Performance in English and Mathematics.* Belfast: Department for Education, Northern Ireland. www.deni.gov.uk/no_52_2010.pdf

Montie, J.E., Xiang, Z. and Schweinhart, L.J. (2006) Preschool experience in 10 countries: cognitive and language performance at age 7. *Early Childhood Research Quarterly,* 21, 313–331.

NESS (2005) *Early Impacts of Sure Start Local Programmes on Children and Families. Surestart Report 13.* London: DFES. www.ness.bbk. ac.uk/impact/documents/1183.pdf

NESS (2010) The impact of Sure Start Local Programmes on child development and family functioning: report of the longitudinal study of 5-year-old children and their families. London: DfE. www. education.gov.uk/publications/eOrderingDownload/DFE-RR067.pdf

NESS (2012) The impact of Sure Start Local Programmes on seven year olds and their families. Research Report DFE-RR220. London: DfE. www.education.gov.uk/publications/eOrderingDownload/DFE-RR220.pdf

OECD (2011) PISA 2009 Results: Vols II and IV. Paris: OECD. www.oecd. org/document/61/0,3343,en_2649_35845621_46567613_1_1_1_1,00. html

Ramey, C.T., Campbell, F.A., Burchinal, M. *et al.* (2000) Persistent effects of early childhood education on high-risk children and their mothers. *Applied Developmental Science,* 4, 2–14.

Sammons, P., Sylva, K., Melhuish, E.C., Siraj-Blatchford, I., Taggart, B. and Elliot, K. (2002) *The Effective Provision of Pre-school Education Project, Technical Paper 8a: Measuring the impact on children's cognitive development over the pre-school years.* London: Institute of Education/DfES.

Sammons, P., Sylva, K., Melhuish, E., Siraj-Blatchford, I., Taggart, B. and Hunt, S. (2008) *Influences on Children's Attainment and Progress in Key Stage 2: Cognitive Outcomes in Year 6.* London: DCSF. www. education.gov.uk/publications/eOrderingDownload/DCSF-RR048.pdf

Schweinhart, L.J., Barnes, H. and Weikhart, D. (1993) *Significant Benefits: The High/Scope Perry Pre-School Study through Age 27.* Ypsilanti, MI: High/Scope Press.

Shonkoff, J. and Phillips, D. (eds) (2000) *From Neurons to Neighborhoods: The Science of Early Childhood Development.* Washington, DC: National Academy Press.

Siraj-Blatchford, I., Sylva, K., Taggart, B., Sammons, P., Melhuish, E. and Elliot, K. (2003) *The Effective Provision of Pre-School Education (EPPE) Project, Technical Paper 10: Intensive Case Studies of Practice across the Foundation Stage.* London: DfEE/Institute of Education, University of London.

Siraj-Blatchford, I., Sylva, K., Taggart, B., Melhuish, E. and Sammons, P. (2005) The Effective Provision of Pre-School Education Project: findings from the pre-school period. In E. Hammes-Di Bernardo and S. Hebenstreit-Mulkler (eds) *Innovationsprojekt Fruhpadagogik. Professionalitat im Verbund von Praxis, Forschung, Aus-und Weiterbildung* (Vol. 10). Baltmannsweiler, Germany: Schneider Verlag Hohengebren GmbH. Baltmannsweiler, pp. 72–86.

Sylva, K., Melhuish, E., Sammons, P., Siraj-Blatchford, I. and Taggart, T. (2004) *Effective Pre-school Provision.* London: Institute of Education.

Sylva, K., Melhuish, E., Sammons, P., Siraj-Blatchford, I. and Taggart, B. (eds) (2010) *Early Childhood Matters: Evidence from the Effective Pre-school and Primary Education Project.* London: Routledge.

Sylva, K., Melhuish, E., Sammons, P., Siraj-Blatchford, I. and Taggart. B. (2012) Effective Pre-school, Primary and Secondary Education 3–14 Project (EPPSE 3–14) – Final Report from the Key Stage 3 phase: influences on students' development from age 11–14. Research Report DFE-RR202. London: Department for Education. www.education.gov.uk/publications/eOrderingDownload/DFE-RR202.pdf

Vandell, D.L., Belsky, J., Burchinall, M., Steinberg, L. and Vandergrift, N. (2010) Do effects of early child care extend to age 15 years? Results from the NICHD Study of Early Child Care and Youth Development. *Child Development*, 81, 737–756.

CHAPTER 3

Perceptions of parents

Susan Hay

In the late 1990s, my company Nurseryworks undertook a survey of parents to identify what they wanted from the time their children spent at nursery. We expected them to overwhelmingly prioritise 'sound preparation for school' and 'learning basics of reading and writing'. Instead, parents prioritised 'for my child to have happy memories of nursery', and 'I want them to make lasting friendships'. Even back then, parents identified and wanted a broader experience than a standard curriculum offer, and a deeper sense of well-being for their children, over and above school readiness. They understood that nurseries could offer these things, and we appreciated how vital the relationship and correlation of home and nursery life was to the expectations our parents had of us. These findings renewed our attention and energy towards getting to know parents really well and becoming sensitive to their individual circumstances and inclination to reflect, interchangeably, how their children could thrive within and beyond the nursery.

Since then, there have been a number of formalised research projects which have focused on parent aspirations, preferences and expectations of the early years experience of young children, from around the world, many of which have been published in the *International Journal of Early Years Education*. These projects rightly differentiate between parents' expectations of early years services, and their aspirations for their children. In this chapter, I have pulled together extracts from those papers that I feel can help guide practice today.

Susan Hay

What does research say about the expectations of parents from their child's early years setting?

A study undertaken in Hong Kong in 2004, 'Parents' expectations of pre-school education' (Lan 2004), investigated the response to a similar question to that we had looked at informally at Nurseryworks. The researchers examined parents' expectations through interviews, finding that nursery parents seemed to be less demanding of academic learning and showed more concern about their children learning self-care skills. There was no obvious difference in expectations between parents with high and low education levels themselves in terms of the services they sought for their children.

The issue of parents' expectations for their children was returned to in 2013 when 'Assessing parents' opinions and expectations of nursery education for quality assurance' found that there was also no significant variance between families from different socio-economic groups (Ayodele and Tinuola 2013). The researchers concluded that all parents expect early years services to be the foundation for quality assurance throughout their children's education.

An innovative approach to involve parents was put forward in 1999 by Maggie Robson and Kathy Hunt, where a set of 'core conditions' was suggested for increasing the self-esteem and confidence of parents when faced with understanding early years curricula. The purpose was to help parents to take ownership of their child's early education and therefore seek stronger and smoother relationships with staff.

In 2000, a survey, 'Pre-school education: parents' preferences, knowledge and expectations' (Foot *et al.* 2000), undertaken across almost one thousand parents in Scotland, found that constructive partnerships between early years settings and parents relied on a clear understanding of what parents wanted and expected from the provider. Parents prioritised the safety and care of their children above all else. This being in place in their search for the right provision, they then made a final selection based on the relative value they attached to education, and convenience of location related to their own needs. The researchers concluded that parents' final choice of setting depended upon their local support network, their knowledge of early years education, and their perceived control over available options.

In 2002, 'A way of thinking about parent/teacher partnerships for teachers' (Keys 2002) found that while the value of partnership with parents is universally accepted, promoting it and maintaining it by settings is difficult, partly because the one-to-one relationship between parent and early years educator/carer is assigned, unlike most other relationships in our lives, which we choose ourselves. The common interest is the development of the child, but the strength of the relationship depends heavily on a wider 'fit' between parents' cares and concerns and those of the individual to whom they relate most at nursery. The researchers identified a number of factors: the match between the staff and the parents' culture and values; the societal forces on the family; and how the staff and parents view their roles. A systematic approach to making a success of this relationship is suggested, to enable staff to view events from more than one perspective and help them to monitor their responses to particular instances.

More recently, the concern to engage parents to support the education of young children has grown within the early years sector, partly as a result of the findings of the UK's EPPE study which showed that the home learning environment is a crucial factor in a young child's ability to learn and develop. In a study in 2007, 'Enhancing home-school collaboration through children's expression' (Yuen 2011), children were asked for information and materials that connected to their daily lives and interests. They were then asked to communicate to their parents

Figure 3.1 Morning handover (with kind permission of Bright Horizons Family Solutions)

what they wanted, and how their parents could support them, through drawings and newsletters. This process enabled the researchers to explore how the home/setting collaboration could be improved through children's work.

And what has research found about the aspirations parents have for their children?

In 2007 the government set out its goals for children and young people in *The Children's Plan: Building Brighter Futures* (now archived). The goals included involving parents in their child's learning during their formative early years. The primary aim of the research leading to the plan, 'National survey of parents and children: family life, aspirations and engagement with learning' (Gilby *et al.* 2008), was to provide insights into family attitudes and dynamics so that these could support the well-being, behaviour and learning of children. This included looking at the parenting role, adult–child relationships, parents' engagement in children's learning, and how the aspirations and attitudes of children fitted with parents' views.

Findings included that most parents of young children considered shared family time to be important, although higher income families tended to undertake these activities outside the home. A high number of parents felt that babies and toddlers learn best through listening and being involved in daily activities, rather than through one-to-one attention. But this was not put down to an unwillingness to talk to their child at their level. In the researchers' view this reflected the 'cash rich, time poor' lifestyle of working families. Only a small number of parents were prepared to admit that work was a higher priority than family time. Young children expressed a desire to spend more time with parents, and they also felt less certain that their parents knew or liked their friends. Similarly, some children expressed resentment of how parents seemed to be more concerned with how well they did, rather than how happy they were.

One in eight parents did not feel confident about helping their child with school work, their perception being that their own education was inadequate. However two-thirds of parents acknowledged that they should have a role in supporting their child's learning, with one-fifth feeling that learning should be the sole responsibility of the school or setting. However the 'time poor' issue returned, with most parents recognising they did not support their children's learning regularly. Children felt that their parents knew a lot about their learning, whilst only three in ten parents considered they were very involved.

From this research, the government's *Children's Plan* put forward five principles:

- Government does not bring up children – parents do – so government needs to do more to back parents and families.

- All children have the potential to succeed and should go as far as their talents can take them.

- Children and young people need to enjoy their childhood as well as grow up prepared for adult life.

- Services need to be shaped by and responsive to children, young people and families, not designed around professional boundaries.

- It is always better to prevent failure than tackle a crisis later.

It reflected that the best way to increase the effectiveness of parental involvement should centre on raising the aspirations parents have for their children, which in turn would hopefully raise the aspirations children have for themselves.

This contention was challenged by the Joseph Rowntree Foundation in 'Educational aspirations: how English schools can work with parents to keep them on track' (Gordon 2013). This study concluded that the real challenge was not having the right aspirations, but lacking the knowledge of how to achieve them. It argued that understanding how to achieve their aspirations would lead to increased attainment. Further, the Joseph Rowntree work contested the fashionable belief that providing children with 'inspirational mentors' influenced aspiration levels, arguing that effort is better spent nurturing the aspirations that children already have and helping them to make good choices about their own learning. Hence, keeping aspirations on track, the report suggested, makes more sense than changing aspirations. This finding led the researchers to explore the idea that sometimes children may aspire to something with which their parents are not familiar, concluding that it is more useful (for children) to help parents to understand their child's aspirations.

Largely focused on school-age children, there appears to be no reason why the recommendations need not apply to nursery settings. For example, the report also gives examples of ways in which parents have been helped to become actively involved in the children's learning experience through specific events, as part of new pupils' induction. In one school, each form group takes responsibility for preparing a 'getting to know you meal' attended by parents, teachers and pupils. In other schools parents are required to sign all pieces of homework, creating an opportunity for discussion and reinforcing high expectations and ensuring that parents are more aware of what their children are doing at school.

How can early years settings respond to the research findings?

The research findings above identify some opportunities for early years settings to increase their connection with parents and to develop their partnership for the benefit of the child.

By explaining the softer aspects of the curriculum, for example how the setting supports the child's friendships, and describing ways in which the setting involves children in everyday activities – clearing up after an activity or a meal – the staff would be making a positive contribution to some of the challenges parents face in terms of making the best use of the limited time they have to spend with children, particularly if they work. A greater focus on these aspects of nursery when a prospective parent visits could influence their choice to enrol in a setting.

Tuning-in to the parent, their background and family life before a keyworker is allocated could make a significant difference to the constancy and depth of the partnership with parents. They must 'fit', and proper, purposeful assessment of the 'partners' could bring a great deal of value to the relationship.

Helping children to achieve their own aspirations, which may become apparent in nursery and may be different from those of their parents, presents a useful opportunity to engage parents in the child's learning. This might most effectively be done with the child present, when what they have been doing in nursery is shared at the end of the day. This conversation could include helping parents who have not experienced today's nursery curriculum themselves, to acknowledge that they can learn with their child in nursery and, critically, at home.

References

Ayodele, J. and Tinuola, C. (2013) Assessing parents' opinions and expectations on nursery education for quality assurance. *Journal of Education and Practice*, Vol. 4, No. 5.

Foot, H., Howe, C., Cheyne, B., Terras, M. and Rattray, C. (2000) Pre-school education: parents' preferences, knowledge and expectations. *International Journal of Early Years Education*, Vol. 8, No. 3.

Gilby, N., Hamlyn, B., Hanson, T., Romanou, E., Mackey, T., Clark, J., Trikka, N. and Harrison, M. (2008) Family aspirations and engagement with learning. Department for Children, Schools and Families.

Gordon, D. (2013) Engaging with parents to help pupils achieve aspirations. Joseph Rowntree Foundation.

Keys, C. (2002) A way of thinking about parent/teacher partnerships for teachers. *International Journal of Early Years Education*, Vol. 10, No. 3.

Lan, M. (2004) Parents' expectations of pre-school education. Hong Kong Institute of Education Research Repository.

Robson, M. and Hunt, K. (1999) An innovative approach to involving parents in the education of their early years children. *International Journal of Early Years Education*, Vol. 7, No. 2.

Yuen, L. (2011) Enhancing home-school collaboration through children's expression. *European Early Childhood Education Research Journal*, Vol. 19, No. 1.

Children's well-being

Larissa Pople and
Sonia Mainstone-Cotton

Introduction

It is widely accepted that the quality of children's lives should be one of society's greatest concerns. The UN Convention on the Rights of the Child, which the UK ratified in 1991, sets out all the aspects of children's lives that need to be borne in mind if we are to protect children from harm, provide them with what they need for healthy growth and development, and empower them to participate in decision-making about their own lives.

But how often do we actually ask children, particularly younger children, how happy they are with their lives? How often do we ask them about the things in their lives that are most important in making them happy or unhappy?

Whatever their age, children are entitled to be listened to and to have their views taken into account. This principle is enshrined in the UN Convention on the Rights of the Child in Article 12, which asserts that signatory states should:

> assure to the child who is capable of forming his or her own views the right to express those views freely in all matters affecting the child, the views of the child being given due weight in accordance with the age and maturity of the child.

On this basis, the only reasonable justification for not listening to children's views is if they are not capable of forming their own views or do not want to express a view. Since babies enter the world with the ability to communicate their feelings and wishes through noises and facial expressions, and rare is the occasion that children do not hold a view or preference, there are very few reasons not to listen to children. The challenge rests with adults to make time to do so, and to do so properly.

The Children's Society's well-being research

For a number of years, researchers interested in children's well-being have been concerned with the question of whether it is possible to ask children to answer questions about how their lives are going so that we can measure their self-reported well-being. This would allow us to make meaningful comparisons about differences in well-being between children and over time, which would help us to devise child-centred policies and practice.

At The Children's Society, we firmly believe that it is possible to measure children's self-reported well-being. Since 2005, we have been engaged in a pioneering programme of research to explore well-being from the perspective of children themselves. This work has generated a set of self-reported measures that can be used to monitor differences and changes in children's well-being over time. We have found that it is feasible to measure children's subjective well-being, and there are a good many reasons why we should.

Children's assessments of their lives are important for a number of reasons.

First and foremost, we believe, as do many others, that children's happiness and fulfilment should be a fundamental concern for any society.

Second, asking children for their perspectives on the things in their lives that are most important deepens our understanding of the factors that have the most impact on their lives, with some unexpected findings.

Our well-being research is rooted in thousands of conversations with children in which we have explored their ideas about what things contribute to, and what things prevent, a good life for children. Sometimes children's views and opinions about the most important influences on their lives come as no surprise to adults. But this is not always the case. Concepts of children's well-being that have not benefited from the insights of children run the risk of overlooking important areas that have not occurred to adults.

Third, asking children about their lives as a whole, and specific aspects of their lives, reveals that some children are faring much better than others. Our research shows that certain groups of children – for example, those who are disabled or have difficulties with learning, those who live in low income families and those who do not live with their family – are less happy with their lives as a whole and particular aspects of their lives than others their age. Our research also suggests that certain experiences affect children's well-being. Children who have been bullied or say that their family does not get along well together have, on average, much lower well-being than children not reporting these types of experiences. Findings such as these can help guide parents and professionals to focus on the issues that matter most to children, and the children who are most in need.

Fourth, there is also evidence that children who are not happy with their lives may go on to experience subsequent problems in their lives such as poor mental health. Thus, children's negative assessments of their lives in the present can offer early warning signals of poor well-being further down the line. A greater understanding of links such as these would facilitate the provision of early support to those that need it to prevent problems from taking hold.

Concepts of well-being

It is worth outlining a number of different concepts that are well established in the research literature on well-being. First, there is a common distinction between subjective or 'hedonic' well-being, which focuses on children's happiness with their lives, and psychological or 'eudemonic' well-being, which focuses on children's feelings of fulfilment, growth and development.

Secondly, there is a further distinction between two components of subjective well-being – children's emotions or 'affect', such as happiness, sadness or anger, which are typically quite variable, and children's cognitive assessments of how happy they are with their lives overall or different aspects of their lives. Emotions have a momentary quality – you may feel happy one moment, but sad the next. Indeed, in our research we have found that children are, on average, slightly happier on weekend days. In comparison, cognitive assessments are fairly stable. Figure 4.1 shows children's responses to three different questions about their well-being on different days of the week – feeling happy yesterday (emotional/affective), feeling satisfied with life as a whole (cognitive), and feeling that life is worthwhile (psychological).

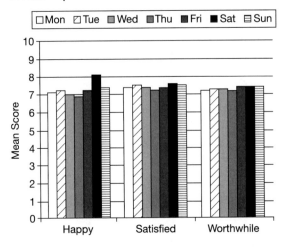

Figure 4.1 Children's well-being on different days of the week

Most of our research at The Children's Society has focused on children's cognitive assessments of their happiness with their lives as a whole and their happiness with different aspects of their lives. We know that children aged eight and above are able to answer these types of questions about their well-being. However, there are cognitive limits to these types of questions and so they are less suitable for young children. Questions about emotions, on the other hand, are easier for young children to understand and relate to concepts that are familiar, partly because they are central to the Early Years Foundation Stage. We have done some initial exploration of the potential for developing simple measures of well-being for younger children (see later sections), but more research is needed in this area.

Different aspects of well-being

We have developed an index of children's well-being – the Good Childhood Index – which asks children about the ten aspects of their lives with the greatest influence on their well-being (see the box opposite). This short index of well-being has been designed to measure trends and variations in children's subjective well-being at the national level. It was tested with a representative sample of 8 to 15 year olds in 2010, and shows good stability and validity (Rees *et al.* 2010). Since 2010, we have been using this index to monitor children's well-being every three to six months in a household survey of 2,000 8 to 15 year olds. We also included the Good Childhood Index questions in a national schools survey of

8 to 15 year olds that we carried out in 2010/11. As a result we now have a large and nationally representative dataset of information on children's well-being, which has involved over 30,000 children.

There are some interesting patterns in children's assessments of how these aspects of their lives are going. First, children tend to rate some aspects of their lives more positively than others. Children are most happy with their relationships with family and friends, their health and their home, and least happy with their prospects for the future and the amount of choice that they have in life.

For most of the Good Childhood Index items, children become less happy as they move into their early teenage years, as can be seen in Figure 4.2. For example, 8 and 9 year olds are much happier with their appearance, school and money/possessions than 14 and 15 year olds. In contrast, happiness with friendships remains consistently high across the age range.

The Good Childhood Index comprises the following questions:

Please say how much you agree or disagree with each of the sentences:
(Strongly disagree to strongly agree scale)

My life is going well
My life is just right
I wish I had a different kind of life
I have a good life
I have what I want in life[1]

How happy are you with . . .
(0–10 scale where 0 = 'very unhappy' and 10 = 'very happy')

. . . your life as a whole?[2]
. . . your relationships with your family?
. . . your relationships with your friends?
. . . the home you live in?
. . . the school you go to?
. . . your health?
. . . your appearance?
. . . the way that you use your time?
. . . how much choice you have in life?
. . . the things you have (like money and the things you own)?
. . . what may happen to you later in your life (the future)?

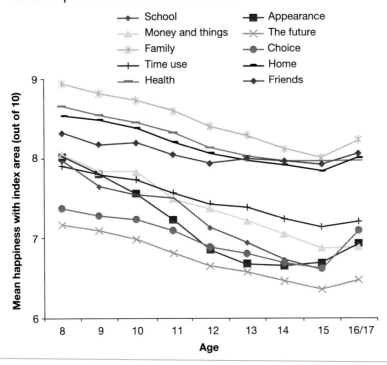

Figure 4.2 Age differences for items in the Good Childhood Index

There are also gender differences for some of the Good Childhood Index items, most notably for appearance and school. Boys, especially younger boys, are less happy with school than girls. On the other hand, girls, especially older girls, are much less happy with their appearance than boys.

In terms of the aspects of life that contribute most to children's overall well-being, three of the Good Childhood Index items stand out as being the most influential – family relationships, choice, and money/possessions. One way to illustrate this is to look at how these aspects of life are related to the likelihood of children having low well-being.[3] For example:

● Children who said that their family does not 'get along well together' were eight times more likely to have low well-being.

● Children who said that they do not 'feel free to express their ideas and opinions' were six times more likely to have low well-being.

● Children reporting having 'a lot less money than their friends' were three times more likely to have low well-being.

Our research has consistently found family relationships to be of fundamental importance to children's well-being. In our qualitative research, children have described in their own words that their family relationships are central to how happy they are with their lives, and that they want to have loving, supportive and harmonious family relationships on the one hand, while being granted a reasonable level of choice and autonomy on the other. Children's comments are supported by our survey research, in which we have found three dimensions of family relationships to be especially important: family harmony, support and autonomy-granting.[4] Figure 4.3 shows how children who report low support, autonomy and harmony in their family relationships have significantly lower well-being than their peers (The Children's Society 2013a).

Choice and autonomy are recurrent themes in our research with children. Our survey research shows a marked drop in happiness with choice between the ages of 8 and 15, but we know from qualitative research that choice and autonomy are important topics for young children too. For example, young children have told us that they would like to make choices regarding their free time, clothes, food, lessons at school and future career options.

Children's happiness with their money and possessions is another aspect of the Good Childhood Index that has been shown to have a strong influence on their overall well-being. In particular, our research has demonstrated that a child-centred approach to measuring poverty and

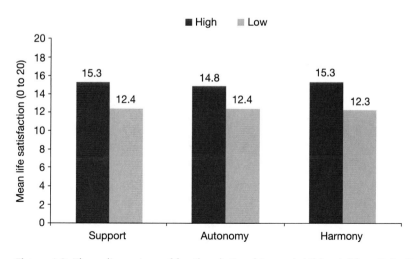

Figure 4.3 Three dimensions of family relationships and children's life satisfaction

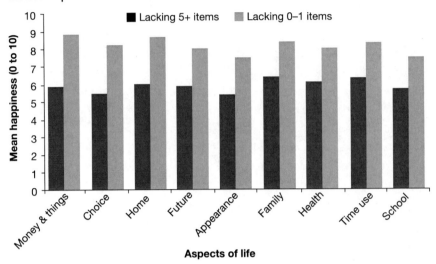

Figure 4.4 Difference in happiness with different aspects of life between materially deprived children and non-deprived children

deprivation yields much stronger links with well-being than more traditional measures such as household income.

As can be seen in Figure 4.4, children lacking five or more items from our child-centred index of material deprivation have significantly lower happiness with every aspect of life in the Good Childhood Index than children lacking none or one of the items.

Policy and practice

Many of the issues that have been raised in our well-being research with children are amenable to both national and local policy interventions.

We have outlined some of the ways in which policy makers could take children's well-being into account (The Children's Society 2012b). Our framework, which is shown in Figure 4.5, is based on six key factors which have been identified by the Office for National Statistics as directly influencing people's well-being (Beaumont 2011).

There is also potential for local initiatives to improve the quality of children's lives. In recent years, we have been working with a number of local authorities, and hundreds of schools, to design and undertake surveys of children within their locality that can provide information on different aspects of children's lives. The findings from these surveys can then be fed into strategic planning and local policy initiatives in relation to children and young people.

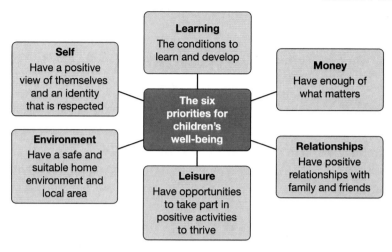

Figure 4.5 Six priorities for children's well-being

Our work on the Isle of Wight is one such example. In 2012 we carried out a well-being survey and follow-up face-to-face consultations with about 5,000 children on the island. We were able to compare the results of the Isle of Wight survey with our national findings to see how children on the Isle of Wight were faring in comparison to national averages. We were then able to undertake further more detailed analysis and consultation with children in respect of the aspects of life where they appeared to be faring worse – school and appearance. This generated some concrete evidence to inform local policy and practice (The Children's Society 2013b).

Exploring well-being with five to seven year olds

Children are never too young to inform adults of their views and feelings. The importance of this is acknowledged and recognised by Alderson (2008: 25), who suggests that children's participation rights are sometimes viewed as contentious because some adults believe children are too young to have an opinion or too young to inform adults of their views. At The Children's Society we are clear that all the children we work with are able to inform us about the things that are important in their lives and about how they are feeling, regardless of age.

There is a growing research literature about the importance of listening to children, with a number of advocates highlighting the need to listen to young children in particular. Lancaster (2003) and Clark and

Moss (2011) have led the way in promoting ways to listen to young children, and have helped to inform our practice and understanding at The Children's Society. Their emphasis on recognising that children are never too young to inform us of how they view the world has been an important guiding principle for us.

As mentioned earlier, most of our research on well-being has been with children aged eight and above, and the types of questions that we ask, which relate to children's cognitive assessments of how happy they are with their lives, are less suitable for younger children. Furthermore, the way in which we ask these questions – i.e. through surveys – is more suited to older children. Researchers have argued that children younger than seven do not have the cognitive skills to be able to answer survey questions (de Leeuw 2011). However others have shown that it is possible to ask children as young as four about their views on different aspects of their lives, provided that the questions are presented in a format that they understand (Thompson *et al.* 2014). Interestingly, research reveals that there is often a lack of agreement between children's own responses to self-report questions and proxy reports given by their parents (Davis *et al.* 2007). This suggests that children have a different perspective from their parents that it is important to capture. Whilst acknowledging that young children may struggle to answer self-report questions about their lives for a number of reasons, we believe that it is important to find ways of helping them do so, and that self-reports from children should always be valued.

Longitudinal research with children, such as the Millennium Cohort Study, provides an interesting source of data on the influences on young children's well-being. Now that the cohort of children involved in the Millennium Cohort Study have reached their middle childhood years, it will be possible to analyse the links between children's early experiences, as reported by adults, and their self-reported well-being at age 11 (The Children's Society, forthcoming). This is likely to offer some interesting insights into the role of early years care and education in relation to children's longer-term well-being.

There are a number of key processes to consider when assessing whether children at a particular stage of their development are able to answer questions about themselves in surveys. The key processes involved in answering survey questions are described as follows:

- First, children have to make sense of the question and determine the intended meaning, so children's *language development* and *compre-hension* are important.

- Next, they have to recall relevant information from their *memory* to come up with an initial response.

- Then they have to formulate an answer either in words (if the research is qualitative) or by choosing a response category (if the research involves a survey). 'Social desirability' can play a role here. It is argued that younger children are especially keen to please and to go along with what adults say (Borgers *et al.* 2000).

Various strategies could be used to address some of these issues, for example:

- using one-to-one interviews or audio recordings with pictures so that children do not have to read the questions themselves;

- ensuring that the questions are short, clear and simply worded;

- asking about concrete concepts that younger children can comprehend, and only about the present not the future or past;

- giving simple response categories, e.g. yes or no, or a limited number of smiley faces.

We wanted to explore these ideas with children under eight and hear their ideas about the things that are important to them. With these things in mind, in 2011 we carried out a focus group with a group of six year olds to explore the following key themes:

- Children's own ideas about the things in their lives that are most important to them, and the things that make them happy, sad, angry, nervous, excited and surprised. As far as possible, we tried to ensure that their ideas were not influenced or circumscribed by us.

- The words and phrases that children use to describe the things that are important to them. This would help us to select simple, age-appropriate language that children their age are likely to understand.

- The ways in which children are influenced by each other and by adults when making decisions as to how to respond to questions about their well-being.

- Children's preferences for different ways of answering questions about their well-being, and the limits to their attention span.

We used a puppet to explore children's understandings of different emotions (e.g. happy, sad, excited, angry, relaxed, scared, worried, full of energy, lonely) and what might make children have these feelings.

We then asked children to draw pictures of the things that make children happy, the things that make children sad, and what they would wish for if they could.

Food featured highly in their drawings and comments, both in terms of their favourite foods and the foods that they did not like. The way they talked about food suggested that it was an important issue for choice and autonomy. As one boy stressed

I hate trying new foods.

Leisure activities were another common theme, including playing outside, going to the park, playing football, colouring, playing on the computer and watching television. Again, choice and autonomy emerged as an important issue.

I love going outside.

And when might you not be able to go outside then?

When it's raining . . . I love raining!

So you'd like to go outside when it's raining and put on a jacket and just get wet?

I wish I didn't even have a jacket! I like splashing in puddles!

Several of the children mentioned their family in relation to the things that they 'love'. There was also discussion of both the positive and negative aspects of having siblings. One of the boys said that he didn't like playing with his sisters, while two of the other children said that they wished they had some/more siblings.

I love my mum and dad and chocolate . . .

I wish . . . I had a brother and sister and I don't have any.

Children understood all the emotions that we asked them about. When we asked them about the sorts of things that might make them feel 'sad' or 'worried', they mentioned a number of things related to family including not having a home or losing a family member. The theme of being lost, abandoned or away from parents emerged a number of times.

Q. Why might Lily (the puppet) be sad?
    Because she hasn't got a home.

Q. Why might Lily be worried?
    That their dad was gone.
    She's lost her family.
    Like if you are an adult or just a kid but bigger then you didn't have any mum and dad and you were walking somewhere then you'd be really worried because no one could look after you . . .
    If you were alone and nobody could adopt you and nobody liked you . . . that could make you a little bit upset . . .

Similar themes came up in relation to friends. Children talked about being alone, not having anyone to play with and being left out of other children's games.

Why might Lily be sad?

Because she's got no friends.

Because nobody wants to play with her.

Because she's got . . . beaten up and she's all alone.

Why might Lily be angry?

Because her friends were being mean to her.

Or they laugh at her and they say 'she looks funny'.

Exploring well-being with under-fives

We know from research that it is important to recognise the importance of well-being right from the beginning of childhood. We also know from research on brain development that different styles of parenting can have an effect on the baby's brain system and development. Children need to have loving and receptive parents who are able to respond to their needs. Sunderland (2006: 22) describes how parents need to be emotionally responsive to the child so that the child's brain can form vital connections that will enable them to cope well with stress later on in life and to have a better sense of well-being.

We know from experience and through the work of Clark and Moss (2011) and Lancaster (2003) that an essential element of listening to younger children is the use of creative methods. The work in Reggio Emilia has led the way across the world in demonstrating that children express themselves through hundreds of different languages. The role of adults is to enable children to express themselves through many different ways. We have used these ideas to ensure that our work with the youngest of children is creative and imaginative, and that we are open to the many different ways children want to express their thoughts and feelings.

However this cannot be rushed. Rinaldi (2005: 20) reminds us that listening takes time, and that we need to allow for silences and long pauses. She also proposes that we need to be curious and interested.

When we have explored the well-being of younger children, we have needed to adapt some of our methods. Recognising that it can be intimidating for younger children to work with people that they do not know, we have tended to use experienced early years researchers alongside practitioners who already have a good relationship with the children. A vital element of our approach is to go at the child's pace and to be playful.

We have used a variety of creative methods to capture children's ideas and thoughts about well-being. These have included:

- Drawing/painting – we have asked children to draw or paint something that makes them happy or sad. It is important to make sure that there are good pens and paint for the children to use. This indicates that this is something special and that we value what the children are making. When the child has finished the drawing we ask them what their picture is about. We usually take a photo of the picture so the child can take the picture home with them if they want to.

- Playdough/plasticine – we have asked children to make a model of something that makes them happy or sad. We then ask the child about this, finding out what they have made, and what their feelings are about it. Again, we usually take photos of the model so that the child can take it home with them if they want to.

- Cameras/videos – we have asked children to take photos or a video of the things that make them happy or sad. We then talk to them about the photos or film that they have made and why. Again, the child may want copies of the photos or film to take home with them.

- Photo story books – we have used these simple books as a way of finding out from children their thoughts and feelings. We write a very simple story using photos and questions to introduce a theme that we want to explore. We use the story to explore the theme with the children and at the end of each page we ask them a question, e.g. who can you talk to when you are feeling sad? We often use this with small groups of children.

- Observations – if a child is under two we can still capture their voice by observing them. It is better when this is done by a practitioner who knows the child well, preferably a key person. Observations can inform us of a wealth of information about how the child is feeling and their likes and dislikes.

As part of The Good Childhood Inquiry, we carried out five well-being activities with younger children on the themes of family and friends. One group was with four to six year olds, and four groups were with three to five year olds.

A key theme to emerge from these activities is that spending time playing with their friends and family makes them happy. Children do not appear to mind where they play, or what they play; it is the experience of playing with others that is important. Friends could be of any age, family members, siblings or pets.

Even from a very young age, children recognised their role in a happy family.

Being good
Being kind
Being friendly

(group of four to six year olds)

My Mummy makes me happy. I cuddle her.

(group of three to five year olds)

On the other hand, arguments with friends emerged as a key concern for this age group.

How do you feel when you argue with your friends?
Sad.
Sad, if someone don't like you, you need to go home and tell mum and dad.

(group of three to five year olds)

Conclusion

At The Children's Society we have explored a number of aspects of well-being with children – including their emotions, their happiness with their lives as a whole and different aspects of their lives, and their sense of fulfilment and purpose.

Key themes to emerge from our research with young children are the importance of play, good relationships with friends and family, and also a level of choice and autonomy to do the things that they would like to do. Helping young children to develop their emotional vocabulary and understanding is fundamental to understanding their well-being. We recognise the importance of working with children to identify how they are feeling and to help them express this from an early age. In our children's centres our experienced practitioners regularly talk to children about how they are feeling and introduce an emotional vocabulary through using images, stories, words, and puppets. The role of adults listening to children when they express their feelings and thoughts is vital. Adults need to be able to listen to and empathise with children while also helping them to explore and understand how they feel.

All children are entitled to be asked about their well-being – and listened to when they respond. This principle is enshrined in rights frameworks, which highlight children's entitlements, whatever their age, to be listened to and to have their views taken into account. It is for adults to create a culture of listening to children from a young age. If children are supported to develop the skills that they need to express themselves from a young age, this will help as they grow older.

Exploring and measuring children's well-being also has practical use for practitioners and policy makers. Our work with schools and local authorities has shown that well-being research helps local services to better understand the well-being of children within their care. The challenge for adults is not just to *hear from* children directly, but to *listen and act upon* what they hear to improve children's well-being.

Notes

1   This was derived from a measure developed by Scott Huebner in the US. See Huebner (1991).
2   This was derived from a measure developed by Robert Cummins in Australia. See Cummins and Lau (2005).
3   By 'low well-being' we mean those children scoring below the mid-point of a scale, in this case 10 out of 20.
4   The questions about family harmony were: 'Members of my family talk nicely to one another'; 'My family gets along well together'; 'There are not a lot of arguments in my family'; 'Frequency of quarrelling with parent(s)'. The questions about parental support were: 'If I have a problem, my parents will help me'; 'If I am upset or unhappy, my parents spend time listening to me'; 'My parents listen to my views and take me seriously'; 'Frequency of talking to parent(s) about things that matter'. The questions about parental autonomy-granting were: 'My parents are too strict'; 'My parents try to control how I live my

life'; 'My parents like me to make my own decisions'; 'My parents give me enough freedom'.

References

Alderson, P. (2008) *Young Children's Rights: Exploring Beliefs, Principles and Practice*, 2nd edn. London: Jessica Kingsley Publishers.

Beaumont, J. (2011) Measuring national well-being. Discussion paper on domains and measures. Newport: ONS.

Borgers, N., de Leeuw, E. and Hox, J. (2000) Children as respondents in survey research: cognitive development and response quality. *Bulletin of Sociological Methodology*, 66: 60–75.

The Children's Society (2012a) *The Good Childhood Report: A Review of Our Children's Well-Being*. London: The Children's Society.

The Children's Society (2012b) *Promoting Positive Well-being for Children: A Report for Decision-Makers in Parliament, Central Government and Local Areas*. London: The Children's Society.

The Children's Society (2013a) *The Good Childhood Report 2013*. London: The Children's Society.

The Children's Society (2013b) Isle of Wight survey of children and young people, 2012. London: The Children's Society.

The Children's Society (forthcoming) *The Good Childhood Report 2014*. London: The Children's Society.

Clark, A. and Moss, P. (2011) *Listening to Young Children: The Mosaic Approach*, 2nd edn. London: NCB.

Cummins, R. and Lau, A. (2005) *Personal Wellbeing Index – School Children*, 3rd edn. Melbourne: School of Psychology, Deakin University.

Davis, E., Nicolas, C., Waters, E., Cook, K., Gibbs, L., Gosch, A. and Ravens-Sieberer, U. (2007) Parent-proxy and child self-reported health related quality of life: using qualitative methods to explain the discordance. *Quality of Life Research*, 16, 5: 863–871.

de Leeuw, E.D. (2011) Improving data quality when surveying children and adolescents: cognitive and social development and its role in questionnaire construction and pretesting. Naantali: Department of Methodology and Statistics, Utrecht University.

Huebner, E.S. (1991) Initial development of the Students' Life Satisfaction Scale. *School Psychology International*, 12: 231–240.

Lancaster, P. (2003) *Promoting Listening to Young Children: The Reader*. Maidenhead: Open University Press, Coram Family.

Rees, G., Goswami, H. and Bradshaw, J. (2010) *Developing an Index of Children's Subjective Well-Being in England.* London: The Children's Society.

Rinaldi, C. (2005) Documentation and assessment: what is the relationship? In Clark, A., Kjorholt, A.T. and Moss, P. (2005) *Beyond Listening: Children's Perspectives on Early Childhood Services.* Bristol: Policy Press.

Roberts, R. (2010) *Wellbeing from Birth.* London: Sage Publications.

Sunderland, M. (2006) *What Every Parent Needs to Know.* London: Dorling Kindersley.

Thompson, H.L., Beville M.-C., Price, A., Reynolds, L., Rodgers, L. and Ford, T. (2014) The Quality of Life Scale for Children (QoL-C). *Journal of Children's Services,* 9, 1: 4–17.

Making values visible

Early years in school and early school life

A personal view

Mark Miller

Introduction

I have just been into our reception class and seen children who have been in 'statutory' school for just over a term, sustaining high levels of engagement and concentration in a range of child-initiated activities and adult-led focused tasks, both indoors and outdoors, where sensitive and thoughtful interventions and questioning from adults are challenging and moving children on in their learning. The 'home corner' has been turned into a veterinary practice where 'waiting your turn' is paramount; children are sharing animal story books and information books about pets with parents and other volunteers in the book area; habitats for the class giant land snail are being designed, with thought being given as to how far it moves in a day; a Gruffalo hunt is just beginning outside . . . and it is only ten o'clock in the morning!

Here are some comments from our parents:

No child is invisible.
It feels like the staff really know my child well and this is really important.
The class is a safe and secure environment with wonderfully creative ways to learn.
I love that Robert Blair Primary School is very family oriented and teachers and parents work together to improve the learning of children.

I write at a time when the pace of change in education is unprecedented. Federations, academy chains and free schools are springing up. The locus of control and centralisation of local authorities is vastly diminished.

Figure 5.1 The role play area – veterinary practice

Figure 5.2 SIMS – the giant land snail

Ofsted inspection frameworks are continuously being updated with ever increasing challenges. The New Early Learning Goals (March 2012) for the Early Years Foundation Stage have been introduced and the New National Curriculum 2014 is about to be implemented. While Children's Centres are now firmly established within communities, providing a haven for many children and families, pressures on budgets in some parts of the country are resulting in a shrinking service. In contrast, following Deputy Prime Minister Nick Clegg's 'Making Britain fit for modern families' (2013) speech, the government is now funding new free fifteen-hour places for two year olds from the 40 per cent of poorest families.

Contiguous with all this, the ongoing debate about the optimum statutory age to start school continues to rage; a few months ago 130 early education experts wrote a letter to the *Daily Telegraph* advocating an extension of informal, play-based preschool provision and a delay to the start of formal 'schooling' in England from the current annual intake in the September before the child's fifth birthday until the age of seven (bringing us in line with a number of other European countries who reportedly have higher levels of academic achievement and child well-being).

Significantly, at the same time, at Robert Blair Primary School, we have just opened one of the aforementioned new classes for two year olds under the government's initiative to fund fifteen hours per week of early education and childcare for children from the poorest households. Children will receive high quality early education and care in a safe and stimulating environment supported by qualified early years practitioners. This means that many of these children are commencing their school careers here at Robert Blair Primary School in the term after their second birthday and may well stay with us until they transfer to secondary school at 11 years old.

Of course, the debate is not so much centred on the fact that the children are *in school*, so much as the *types of experiences* they are being offered at each age and stage in their development. There is much research-based evidence which points towards the importance of play in young children's development, and the value of an extended period of playful learning before the start of formal schooling. A good number of studies have claimed better academic, motivational and well-being outcomes for children who attended child-initiated, play-based preschool early education settings. Indeed a play-based preschool education is considered to be of particular advantage to children from disadvantaged households, such as many that we find in the community around Robert Blair Primary School. This view is reiterated in the 4Children Children's Centres Census (2013) which describes Children's Centres as a 'vital resource' to support young children and their families. So let me make it quite clear from the outset: our children, at Robert Blair Primary School, experience learning through a play-based curriculum from the moment they arrive in school – whether at six months, two, three or four years old – which continues well into Year 1 and increasingly beyond that.

School vision and context

Robert Blair Primary School is an inclusive learning community where expectations are high, individuals are nurtured and creativity is valued.

It is a happy, friendly, hard-working one-form-entry primary school in a generously proportioned three-storey building with approximately 270 children on its roll, located just off the lively community of the Caledonian Road (the Cally) in the London Borough of Islington in north London. The school is surrounded by warehouses, factories and studios; the British Transport Police are located next door, Pentonville Prison is at the end of the road.

We support many vulnerable families and are well supported in return by many families who are loyal to the school and appreciative of the opportunities afforded to their children. Almost half of our children come from the Caledonian Ward, one of the 20 per cent most disadvantaged wards in the country. Over 75 per cent are deemed to be from disadvantaged backgrounds. Currently a little under 60 per cent of children are entitled to free school meals. The school community is diverse with just over thirty differently defined ethnic groups. Under 50 per cent have English as a first language and over twenty-five different languages and dialects are spoken.

Evidence from pre-nursery home visits and early observations tells us that attainment on entry to the school is very low; the majority of children start in our nursery class in the term after their third birthday at levels well below national expectations, with particularly poor language, vocabulary and social skills. An increasing number of children transfer from our Children's Centre services into our nursery class. These children are already experienced members of the school community. They can see, and occasionally wander into, the nursery class; they share an outdoor space with their three and four year old peers; they join in with special 'under-fives' events. They are far more likely to be starting

EYFSP results 2012/13

	Communication and language		
	%≥ Age Related Expectations on entry to nursery	3% (1)	
		with LCR	without LCR
1	Emerging	52%	46%
2	Expected	41%	46%
3	Exceeding	7%	8%
	% of children who have accessed Children's Centre Services scoring 2/3	78.5%	

	Physical development		
	%≥ARE on entry to nursery	12% (4)	
		with LCR	without LCR
1	Emerging	28%	19%
2	Expected	69%	77%
3	Exceeding	3%	4%
	% of children who have accessed Children's Centre Services scoring 2/3	71%	

	Personal, social and emotional development		
	%≥ARE on entry to nursery	6% (2)	
		with LCR	without LCR
1	Emerging	34%	27%
2	Expected	66%	73%
3	Exceeding	0%	0%
	% of children who have accessed Children's Centre Services scoring 2/3	74%	

	Literacy						
	%≥ARE on entry to nursery	6% (2)					
		with LCR			without LCR		
	Strands		reading	writing		reading	writing
1	Emerging	62%	62%	62%	58%	58%	68%
2	Expected	28%	21%	24%	31%	23%	27%
3	Exceeding	10%	17%	14%	11%	19%	15%
	% of children who have accessed Children's Centre Services scoring 2/3	91%					

Figure 5.3 Early Years Foundation Stage progress data

Mathematical development						
%≥ARE on entry to nursery	9% (3)					
	with LCR			without LCR		
Strand		number	SSM		number	SSM
1 Emerging	55%	55%	48%	50%	50%	42%
2 Expected	42%	38%	45%	46%	42%	50%
3 Exceeding	3%	7%	7%	4%	8%	8%
% of Children who have accessed Children's Centre Services scoring 2/3	91%					

Understanding the world		
%≥ARE on entry to nursery	6% (2)	
	with LCR	without LCR
1 Emerging	55%	50%
2 Expected	45%	50%
3 Exceeding	0%	0%
% of children who have accessed Children's Centre Services scoring 2/3	85%	

Expressive arts and design		
%≥ARE on entry to nursery	21% (7)	
	with LCR	without LCR
1 Emerging	38%	30%
2 Expected	55%	62%
3 Exceeding	7%	8%
% of children who have accessed Children's Centre Services scoring 2/3	87.5%	

Figure 5.3 *(Continued)*

in the nursery class within the nationally typical development band of 30 to 50 months.

Islington's only Language and Communication Resource (LCR) is based in the school, funded for twenty-four children who have statements of Special Educational Needs, with identified specific speech and language delay or impairment as their primary need. They are on the roll in classes across the school. In addition to this, we have an above average number of statemented children, and a higher than average number of children have social, emotional and behavioural needs. In 2011 the Art Room charity set up its first London base in the school to help us in supporting these children, and it has helped us to value the creativity of children who have not had the advantage of a books-led learning environment at home. Our approach is to:

- teach in a creative way using a series of planned cross-curricular themes, making natural links between subjects;

- develop creativity through the use of the arts as a vehicle for teaching, for example using drama to explore aspects of life in the rainforest; using movement and dance to teach the water cycle or aspects of maths – rotation, shape and space, symmetry;

- ensure that every child, during every academic year, will have at least one opportunity to work 'hands on' on an extended project with an artist/musician/dancer/writer;

- plan for different learning styles;

- provide a variety of recording opportunities as well as writing and mark-making; photos, drawings, mind maps, diagrams, PowerPoint, etc.

- rent space to arts organisations in the school building and make full use of their expertise and facilities.

The school is led and managed by the headteacher, who has a strong early years background and who has been in post for over ten years, bringing stability after a difficult and unsettled period in the life of the school. He is ably supported by a deputy headteacher, a school business manager, an inclusion manager and the under-fives manager. The under-fives manager has day-to-day responsibility for managing the Children's Centre and the Early Years Foundation Stage. Each member of the leadership team is an expert in their field and trusted to manage their area of the school according to the school improvement plan and other agreed policies. All under-fives services, including a parents'/training room, are housed on the ground floor of the school.

Over the last ten years the school has been inspected under three different Ofsted inspection frameworks. Although the whole-school judgements have been variable, the Early Years Foundation

Stage judgements have remained constant, as demonstrated by the following:

> Teaching in the Foundation Stage is consistently strong … the curriculum in the Foundation stage provides pupils with a range of interesting and fun activities and enables them to make good progress.
>
> (2006)

> Children experience a good range of stimulating activities in the Early Years Foundation Stage because it provides a rich and vibrant learning space and teaching is good … highly personalised individual planning for pupils' needs translates into engaged children who make consistent strides in their learning.
>
> (2009)

> Children make a good start in the Early Years Foundation Stage due to consistently well planned teaching.
>
> (2013)

The grounding that we offer our children in the early years stages has led to increasing success as they progress through the school.

Typically we have up to about 130 children in the Early Years Foundation Stage, led and managed by the under-fives manager, who has Qualified Teacher Status and has previously had experience in working as an early years adviser. She is supported by three other teachers and fifteen early years workers spread across our under-fives area in the baby room, toddler rooms, nursery class and reception class.

The Children's Centre services

In 2005, working with the local Children's Centre hub and the local authority Early Years Service, and following some major adaptations to our slightly fading Edwardian-period Greater London Council school building, we set up Children's Centre services in the school and we currently provide all-year-round childcare for nine babies and twenty-four toddlers, wrap-around and holiday care for children up to eight, together with a small selection of family training sessions. We appointed a workforce of mainly experienced early years workers, some qualified, some not. They are all still with us. Many have taken the opportunity to gain further level 2 or level 3 qualifications; two have completed the Foundation degree. Several have been on maternity leave and returned, in some cases bringing their babies with them to our baby and toddler rooms.

Figure 5.4 Baby room

Figure 5.5 Toddler room

Further significant building adaptations took place in the summer of 2012 to facilitate the opening of a second toddler room under the government's scheme to provide fifteen hours of early education and childcare for children from poorer homes. Two experienced staff moved from our nursery class to work in this room together with a newly appointed member of the under-fives team.

Our original baby and toddler rooms attracted families from a wider area beyond the immediate local school community, who were looking for childcare in order for parents to return to work or study. Islington has a subsidised scheme so that families will be charged on a sliding scale according to their family income, and priority is given to residents from within the borough. An increasing number of these families chose to transfer their children into our nursery class and to continue to take advantage of the wrap-around care that we provide before and after school and during school holidays. A number also chose to apply for places in our reception class, though as the popularity of the school has grown, many of these parents have been unsuccessful and have therefore taken school places nearer to their homes. We have been sad to say goodbye to children and families who have sometimes already been with us for four years by that time; a significant investment of time and emotion for both sides.

We now have a scattering of children throughout most of the school who started with us as babies or toddlers. Over the years we have supported their parents through 'stay and play' sessions; family first aid; introductions to messy play; story sacks; helping your child at home with reading, with maths, with science; cooking on a budget in our 'family kitchen'; Bengali mums' sewing and gardening; to mention but a few.

The 4Children Children's Centres Census (2013) points out that Children's Centres have a clearly defined core purpose which is to 'improve outcomes for children and their families and reduce inequalities between families in the greatest need and their peers', through:

- promoting child development and 'school readiness' (there is more discussion of 'school readiness' below);

- enhancing parents'/carers' aspirations and parenting skills;

- improving child and family health and life chances.

Where a *primary school* is additionally providing early education and childcare places, we would add the following benefits:

- getting to know the child and family really well over time;

- a joined-up, consistent and long-term view of a child's learning journey;

- a cumulative sharing of information about the child's development;

- early identification and ongoing intervention for any special needs the child may have;

- early identification and ongoing support for any needs within the family;

- an extended relationship with the family.

All of which make a positive difference to the child's academic achievement and well-being.

The nursery class

Most children move from our toddler room to our 52 full-time-equivalent-place nursery class which currently has 42 full-time (school day) places, and 20 part-time places of fifteen hours, usually spread over two and a half days. There are two nursery teachers and three early education workers. Each member of staff is keyworker for a group of, usually, twelve children.

The classroom is a large, bright and busy L-shaped space with a kitchen at one end, and a 'homely' area with sofas and floor cushions leading into creative areas, role play areas, a book corner, writing area, number area, construction, small world, and so on. There is continual access to two different areas of the outdoor space.

Children join our nursery class at the beginning of the term after their third birthday. For the majority this is their first time in school, though a small number transfer from our Children's Centre services and one or two come from other early years settings. From the beginning we aim to capture children's imagination and stimulate their curiosity. By providing opportunities for our children to learn in a variety of ways, through all their senses, we encourage them to develop as independent and enthusiastic thinkers.

Play is central to children's learning in the Foundation stage. Children's learning, indoor and outdoor, is supported through planned play, using the six areas of learning of the Early Years Foundation Stage:

- Communication and language

- Physical development

- Personal, social and emotional development

- Literacy

- Mathematics

- Understanding the world

- Expressive arts and design.

Staff plan activities and experiences, both indoors and outdoors, that support children's individual stages of development and reflect their interests. Adults also observe and join in with children's spontaneous play to extend and develop their learning.

The vast majority of the children make the seamless transfer from the nursery class to our reception class. Two or three in each cohort may transfer to local faith schools or are unable to secure a place because they live too far from the school.

The reception class

Our reception class is based in a light and airy corner of the school building in a space originally designed to accommodate forty-five children, with immediate access to a veranda and outdoor space beyond. It is physically right next door to the nursery class and close to the toddler rooms, being part of the wider 'under-fives' area of the school. The outdoor space is shared between all the under-fives; though there are designated areas, these are not fenced off and so children can visit younger/older siblings and friends easily. As you would expect, the reception classroom is set up with the usual areas for books, writing, maths, art, construction, role play, snacks, and so on.

Our last two reception teachers have been 'home grown', having spent part of their training at the school, passed their NQT year and gone on to become outstanding teachers of young children. Our longstanding early years worker, together with regular BTEC and PGCE student placements, ably supports them.

We recognise the holistic nature of children's development and learning. We are committed to providing the opportunity for all children, from their earliest years, to develop as learners. We believe that learning is a shared process and that children learn most effectively when, with the support of a knowledgeable and trusted adult, they are actively involved and interested. We know that parents, carers and families are central to the well-being of the child. We aim to support parents and families in this role in a variety of ways.

The staff use the curriculum to plan activities and experiences that support children's individual stages of development and reflect their interests. Play is central to children's learning and so learning, whether it takes place indoors or outdoors, is supported through planned play. As with our nursery class, adults also observe and join in with children's spontaneous play to extend and develop their learning.

The indoor and outdoor areas in the reception class are organised to give the children space to move about safely and easily. Equipment is stored and labelled so that children know where to find things, enabling them to become independent learners. The outdoor area is planned to support learning in all areas of the curriculum. There are some parts of the curriculum that can only be learnt outside, such as changes in seasons and weather and discovering mini-beasts. Outdoor experiences also allow children to work on a larger, more active and exuberant scale than is possible indoors. Children in the reception class have free access to outdoor space throughout the greater part of the day.

The children

The majority of our children arrive in our reception class just before 9 o'clock, although a handful transfer from breakfast club, having arrived any time after 8 o'clock. Parents or carers accompany the children into the classroom where they self-register with their name card and then share a book or begin one of a selection of activities to start the day. As their children settle, the parents gradually leave and the children gather together for carpet time with a story, phonics and chat about the day. Each week four key children are observed, and then during the following week, activities are planned around their individual needs, interests and next steps for learning. Parents or carers are consulted to get as full and accurate a picture as possible.

For example: Zara was new to the school when she started in our reception class and so the following appeared in the teacher's planning notes:

Mark Miller

Interests/schemas, learning needs, CoEL*	New to school, separation from family difficult in the mornings, Zara will say she misses mum. Zara beginning to become more relaxed and play with other children rather than seeking out adults. Loved potion making last week. Enjoys 'princess play' and outdoor sand. Number recognition and application is solid, writing well formed letters and can write her name. Recognises some phonemes and graphemes. Not assertive in group times, but will respond when asked directly.
Parents/carers information	At school she likes making things, sticking, story time, bikes outdoors. At home she likes colouring, cooking, baking, maths. It was Zara's birthday last weekend and it will be Dad's this weekend. Grandparents away for an extended holiday in Bangladesh, she misses them. She needs encouraging to talk clearly, she is happy to play by herself. I would like to know how Zara interacts with other children.
Next steps for learning and development/ support needed from adults	Engage Zara quickly in the morning to reduce upset when separating by asking her to help or play with another child. Ensure art trolley for mixing paint/large mark-making is set up for her to access in the mornings. Adults engage her in talk with other children and to listen out for incorrect pronunciation and correct it. Try noisy neighbour, listening games and talk about the robot made last week and class land snail. Feedback to parents.

* Characteristics of Effective Learning: playing and exploring, active learning, creating, thinking critically to support children's learning

Contrastingly, Micah has been with us since he was just over six months old:

Interests/ schemas, learning needs, CoEL	Use of number and mathematical knowledge is very well developed and he is beginning to extend concepts with a context – investigating length with Unifix, building a marble run, playing table top games, etc. Reads confidently using phonics, enjoys guided reading and stories. Developing control of pen/ pencil using pincer grip, though mark-making still faint. Developing good friendships. Can tell an adult when upset or worried about something.
Parents/carers information	Not returned, though from discussion at parents' evening, parents happy with how he is settled and he enjoys coming to school. He likes playing with his friends outside. Weekends are busy, but they usually go to the park to play on swings, play football, etc. They are concerned about boisterous play at home.
Next steps for learning and development/ support needed from adults	Plan opportunities for investigations – maths capacity and volume. Opportunities to develop fine motor skills – playdough, tweezer games. Mark-making with pencils, experiment with pressure and tone. Provide opportunities for quieter games with friends as well as outdoor play.

Alongside the planning for the four key children each week appears planning for prime areas of learning (personal, social and emotional development, communication and language, physical development) together with specific areas of learning (literacy, maths, understanding of the world, expressive arts and design), and planning for group times and special events. The children to be observed this week and planned for next week are noted and there is space for observations and evaluations of child-initiated play.

Let's meet some of the children (names have been changed):

Sumaya's family had recently arrived as refugees from Afghanistan when she joined the nursery class half-way through the year. She had very limited use of English but since moving into the reception class she is becoming more settled and is making significant improvements in speaking out loud and answering questions. She is very engaged in the life of the classroom and has been observed being focused on one activity for forty minutes or more. She loved the recent partnership work with musicians from the London Symphony Orchestra who came into the school over an extended period, introducing the children to instruments. She has recently moved into the main phonics group having started off in a smaller group for phonics teaching. The school's inclusion manager is monitoring her progress and social/emotional development.

Micah, whom we have already met, is a mixed-race child of professional parents; Mum is a teacher in this school; Dad works in IT. Micah has been with us since he was six months old when his mum returned to work. He is confident and outgoing. The under-fives area of the school is his kingdom; he knows everyone who works there and it is a familiar and secure environment for him. He is one of the minority who entered the reception class at a level in line with national expectations. He loves books. Outdoors is his space of choice, especially where climbing, construction and competition are on the agenda.

Fatma joined our reception class from a local preschool. Mum is concerned about her speech and her friendships. Her family speak Arabic at home. She seems to be unable to form friendships with peers, though she seeks out adults to engage in conversation. She often seems unclear about the task she is undertaking and looks to other children for cues or to adults for reassurance. There are concerns about her lack of progress in all areas, though she loves dressing up and singing. She has been allocated time in a small group with the school's visiting speech and language therapist.

When Jay joined the nursery class he said very little and his vocabulary was limited; his progress since has been slow. He is the youngest of four siblings all now in the school, all brought up solely by mum. Had the free fifteen-hour early education and childcare places for two year olds been available at the time, Jay would have been eligible for a place. He is currently awaiting an operation to have his tonsils and adenoids removed. He will spend long periods of time building in the construction area, talking to himself while other children play around him. He shows no interest in writing/mark-making whatsoever. He has

Figure 5.6 A focus group in reception class

Figure 5.7 Profile books

been identified as one of a small group that the senior early years worker will support for a short time every day in building and using basic vocabulary. His progress will be monitored by the school's inclusion manager.

Every child has a profile book which is started at whatever point they join the school and continues until the end of the Early Years Foundation Stage. Many children accumulate two, three or four volumes during their time with us. It is made up of photographs and observations from key workers together with the child's own drawings, comments and early writing. The profile books are stored so that they are easily accessible to the children and their parents or carers at any time.

Micah has had his profile book since he was six months old and it details his journey through the school with photographs and observations of significant milestones in his development. As well as his key workers, his mum and dad have also contributed photos and narrative to it. Sumaya loves getting her profile book from the shelf and thumbing through the photos of herself and her friends and family, recounting to herself the story of what was going on in the photos she sees.

Partnership with parents

Parents or carers are the child's first educators. There is a large body of research that demonstrates that parents' involvement in their child's education has a positive impact on their development and progress. Many of our children are growing up in deprived neighbourhoods. There is a degree of sensitivity around describing families as 'hard to reach' or 'disadvantaged'. We are more likely to talk in terms of 'supporting needs' or 'working together to improve outcomes for children and families'. As well as signposting families to all the services provided by our local Children's Centre hub, we provide a wide range of opportunities for families based in the school building, which have already been described. Many of these sessions are developed following consultation with parents or even after an informal conversation with an individual parent.

We survey our parents regularly about the work of the school, including specifically the under-fives. Parents are asked simply to tell us:

What do you like about the school?

What is working well?

What difference does this make to your child or family?

What isn't working well?

What could we improve?

What other services would you like to see on offer?

Our usual response rate is 30–40 per cent. Responses tend to be resoundingly positive, though it is the suggested areas for improvement that we find most useful.

In the most recent under-fives survey, strengths could be grouped into six main areas:

- friendliness; a warm welcome and 'family' feel;

- children are happy and settled and gain confidence;

- the effectiveness of key staff and their relationships with adults and children;

- the quality and range of experiences;

- management of behaviour and effective transitions;

- the positive impact of services for children and families on their daily life.

We would regard all of these as standard entitlements and falling within the inspection framework.

Areas for development fell broadly into the following categories:

- communication with parents – more feedback on how children are doing;

- more opportunities for parents and carers to get involved;

- aspects of the physical environment – larger entrance, more green space;

- more enrichment – more outings, access for younger children to after-school clubs;

- extending the service – Saturday opening, longer hours, etc.

At the time of writing, we are working on some of these suggestions, all of which would take us beyond the standard and measured expectations of a primary school.

Our aim in working with families of under-fives is to:

- develop strong social bonds between children, their families, the school and the local community;

- support parents in developing 'positive parenting' and life skills;

- provide good quality, flexible childcare to support parents in returning to volunteering, study or work.

Reflections

Should we adopt the model used in many European countries and delay the start of statutory education to six years or even seven years old?

In many European countries children do not enter formal education until their sixth year, and are still making good if not better progress than their peers in England. But it is also true that many of these European countries have well developed 'kindergarten' systems that children attend from an early age before the start of formal education. The educational system in Denmark, for example, among others, emphasises the links between playful, experiential learning and developmentally sound teaching. Similarly, all agree to some extent that as children develop and mature they will need to engage in more formalised learning activities but that, crucially, this will follow playful learning which has brought them to a point where they are confident, capable, happy, motivated and inspired thinkers and learners.

So, as I said in my introduction, I believe that the real debate is not so much centred on the fact that the children are *in school*, as on the *types of experiences* they are being offered at each age and stage in their development, and consequently the impact that this has on the academic, motivational and well-being outcomes for children. This is probably especially significant for children growing up in poorer families and communities in both rural and inner city locations.

Does a high quality early education and childcare setting improve 'school readiness'?

In our school community, I am convinced it does. This was one of the reasons we set up early education and childcare on our site as soon as the chance was offered to us. Our children come with lower than nationally expected social and cognitive starting points. We wanted to give them the head start that good quality early education and childcare can give, while simultaneously working with their parents or carers to help them better understand how their children learn and how they can help and support them.

By 'school readiness' we mean the development of children's cognitive, behavioural, physical and emotional capabilities. But 'school readiness' is not an end in itself; it should be seen very much in the context of a learning journey, of lifelong learning. One of my favourite quotes from Bruner sums it up adroitly: 'School is not a preparation for life – it is life.'

Government minister Sarah Teather said at the launch of the revised Early Years Foundation Stage that:

> What really matters is making sure a child is able to start school ready to learn, able to make friends and play, ready to ask for what they need and say what they think. These are critical foundations for really getting the best out of school. It's vital we have the right framework to support high quality early years education. Our changes . . . will support early years professionals and families to give children the best possible start in life.

There is no doubt in my mind that those 'foundation years' spent in a high quality nursery provision, and good early education and childcare preceding that, can make a considerable 'school readiness' difference for a lot of children as they enter the reception class. The impact of a well-trained, skilled adult scaffolding a child's learning through considered interactions and collaboration could be second to none. In the case of many of our families, who have limited time and resources for family outings and the like, the difference that this can make is significant.

We regularly see children starting school in our nursery class having attended our baby and toddler rooms who are at least one developmental band further on than most of their peers. Based on our observations of our small cohorts, I would further suggest that these children mostly continue on a more accelerated learning journey through the reception year and beyond than that of their peers who may not catch up until Year 2 or Year 3, if at all.

Does single entry into reception class every September impact on 'school readiness'?

We are all too well aware that children starting school each September are all at very different starting points; that some children are less 'school ready' than others – for example, children born in the summer are entering school a whole year before those who are born after August 31. With single form entry to schools, children may only just be four years old as they enter statutory school. This could then be severely compounded if, say, the child is a summer-born boy, was born prematurely, has special educational needs or is learning a second language. Good quality preschool experience can help, but we have to work much harder to ensure these children succeed.

Is a play-based curriculum important in a reception class?

Yes, yes, yes! It is therefore crucial that the reception class provides continuing opportunities for learning to take place through play. I would argue that for many children this remains the case into Year 1 and beyond. We believe that play and learning are mutually supportive. The place of play in children's thinking and learning is crucial for their progress in all areas but particularly in developing language, for personal, social and emotional development, and in physical development. To cut off these opportunities too early is to stunt their development.

Cathy Nutbrown talked about 'a mischievous mistruth in the belief that doing certain things early helps children get ready for the next stage'. This is what underpins those reception classrooms where every child has a seat and we all write together, we all do maths together and then we choose. But young children learn best by moving about. Young children's learning is a 'whole body experience' and so can be sadly limited by reducing their capacity for movement whilst learning. Young children learn best by 'doing'. Nutbrown went on to say that 'the best way to help a child to get ready to be 5 is to let her be 3 when she is 3 and let him be 4 when he is 4, and to hold high expectations of what children in their first 48 months of life might achieve'. Hurrah!

Taught content versus planning for individual children's interests and needs?

I have already mentioned the educational system in Denmark, which emphasises experiential, investigative and playful learning and the clear and specific links with developmentally sound teaching. Both are necessary for the child's sound development and progress. You have seen how we use and place great importance on observations and information about a child's own interests to plan next steps for their learning. However few children will show an interest in *all* prime and specific areas of learning during their time in the Early Years Foundation Stage. Some aspects of learning will need to be specifically planned for if children are to experience them. Not all children will show an interest in phonics, or how to double or halve a number. Teachers will have to plan specifically taught activities to ensure that all aspects of the Early Learning Goals in the prime areas of learning are covered, so that children attain a 'good level of development'. So a balance between taught content and planning for individual children's interests and needs is paramount.

What are the benefits of having early education and childcare in a primary school?

Having early education and childcare provision based in the school benefits the children and families in our catchment area because we have the opportunity to:

● improve outcomes and reduce inequalities for children and their families;

Figure 5.8 Toddlers' outdoor play

Figure 5.9 Concentration

- identify needs early and support children and families throughout their primary years;

- develop 'school readiness' for those who have less advantaged home learning environments;

- maintain a joined-up, consistent and long-term view of a child's learning journey, and an extended relationship with the family.

Sadly not all of our children and families are able to benefit. Those who can pay and those who are on very low family incomes do. In our area those who do not benefit are still on low incomes, though just above the government threshold. We would to like to see these opportunities extended to everyone within our school community.

Future aspirations: my wish list

- A widening of eligibility to ensure that *all* families in certain disadvantaged school communities can benefit from early education and childcare places, not just the poorest and those who can afford to pay.

- A change to school admission criteria and regulations which would allow parents choosing to send their children to an early years education and childcare setting in a school, to keep their child at the school for statutory schooling from five to eleven years old.

- One funding allocation for Children's Centre services and statutory schooling, nationally and locally, so that we can budget across the whole school to meet the needs of children and their families.

- More Children's Centres based within schools, providing early education and childcare, together with outreach and support for families, creating greater opportunities for integrated working and for centres to extend their work to include over-fives (one of the recommendations of the 4Children Children's Centres Census 2013).

- A national expectation of a play-based approach to children's learning until they are six years old. Schools to be remodelled or designed with this in mind, with generous allocation of indoor and outdoor space.

A final quote from a parent says it all:

There is a family feel, with love and understanding, it gives my son a home-like space to learn and grow with friends together. Without Robert Blair Primary School and childcare we wouldn't be able to keep working. Simple as that!

The indoor environment at work

Helen Huleatt

Introduction

Community Playthings was begun in the United States shortly after the Second World War by a handful of idealistic young couples at a land co-operative in the Appalachian Mountains. One of their goals was to raise the local people's living standards by developing an industry using the most abundant local resource: wood. These couples belonged to the peace movement of that time and wanted a simple standard of living for themselves and their families. They each brought their own angle or experience; one was handy with machinery; my mother was a teacher, etc. Their children tested these new products. It quickly became apparent that children's imagination and creativity are better fostered by simple open-ended play things than by prescriptive toys. This observation strengthened the emphasis on simplicity, which has been a hallmark of Community Playthings ever since, in contrast to 'play' products designed to entertain in a specific way. We are practitioners and we have our own nurseries.

Community Playthings' very first product was created by Caroline Pratt in 1913 at Bank Street College in New York City; she designed the solid wooden block so that its width was twice its height and half its length. Pratt was Froebel-trained, and Froebel's ideas have subsequently been incorporated into all our products. He had much to say about intrinsic motivation, about play, about harmony and about connecting children with nature. He believed that every child is a thought of God and that the educator's task is not to mould the child but rather to try to recognise and support this 'thought' so that each develops and blossoms in his or her own unique way.

The central concept that has guided the work of Community Playthings is the importance of learning from and *observing* children: *how* they interact and learn and *how* they convey their feelings. Every day, our team is immersed in continual observation, analysis and review; we frequently invite child development professionals from across the UK to add their thoughts to the discussions that feed into our ongoing design and literature. It is inspiring work. Just as children continually surprise us with their original thoughts and actions, so I never know what my next assignment will be – the only thing I do know is that it will serve childhood.

Children's ability to thrive has a direct correlation to their physical surroundings. This understanding has been acknowledged through many years and across geographical differences. In Italy's Reggio Emilia nurseries, staff give careful attention to room layout, perceiving the environment itself as a 'teacher'. Two centuries ago in Germany, Friedrich Froebel first envisaged the *Kindergarten*, an inspirational 'garden' where children would blossom. A hundred years later Margaret McMillan adopted his ideas to establish the first British nursery school, saying, 'We are trying to create an environment where education will be almost inevitable.'

Environment reflects ethos

Just as every individual is unique and every culture has its flavour, so each nursery is a distinct entity. Its ethos is expressed through its physical attributes, and its atmosphere is evident to anyone entering. In fact, it has been said that parents decide whether or not to use a setting within five minutes of arrival. So it is vital for leadership and staff to start by considering, 'What do we believe is important for children and their families?'

Anita Olds (2000) wrote, 'It is the spirit of a place that makes it memorable, that expands our sense of possibility and puts us in touch with what is most loving, creative and human about ourselves.' Such spirit can be apparent from the threshold of the front door. It is obvious that staff love their work in settings with imaginative touches throughout. An aesthetically delightful place communicates respect for childhood, for families and for learning. Varying light levels within the room, woven wall hangings, crafted wood furniture, fabrics that soften hard corners, interesting artefacts and natural objects, wicker baskets, and living plants are elements that might give form to this intangible spirit. Any place will make a lasting positive impression if children associate it with happy feelings and warm memories.

As well as expressing the nursery's pedagogy, décor can also create variation within the whole. The same wooden archway might be enhanced with exuberant African fabric in one area of the setting and dreamy pastel gauze in another, supporting a different ambience in each.

Children's focus, communication and learning flourish in child-size spaces where they feel at ease. When furniture is on their scale, children instinctively sense 'This is for me!' Adults recalling their favourite childhood spot often describe a hide-away beneath a special bush or 'under granny's kitchen table', so it is good to include cosy nooks within each room. Children retreating into these secure havens may be processing incoming impressions, preparing to face new situations or 'learning the ropes' by observing their peers (Olds 2000).

Curves – created with furniture, fabric or plants – suggest welcoming open arms and make a room seem friendlier than straight lines and right angles. Natural light, and interplay of light and shadow, help children relax. One Somerset Children's Centre was designed so that rainwater in gutters reflected sunlight through skylights, causing rippling patterns on ceiling and walls. Similar effects might be created by a rattan window screen moving in the breeze.

Time is an ally in the process of preparing a room for children. If one area is developed at a time, each can be given the thought and care it deserves. Creating a beautiful space, like anything worthwhile, takes time.

The whole environment wants to stimulate interest and curiosity – but it should not *over*-stimulate children. Several elements that are beneficial in moderation may be distracting or even exhausting in excess. Sound is one example. Constant background music can be wearing and disturbs children's focus. It is better to share times of listening or singing. In rooms where harsh acoustics cause stress – often due to hard surfaces or high ceilings – fabrics, drapes, cushions and rugs might help alleviate the noise. For a high-ceilinged room to seem less institutional, strings of lights or hanging ferns could be added as well.

Toys and materials in excess lead to clutter. Too much choice overwhelms children and prompts them to flit from one occupation to another without becoming truly engaged. Odds and ends build up in any setting and need to be trimmed back occasionally, because for children, 'less is more'. Fewer materials, attractively arranged, look more cared for and give children a clearer sense of what is on offer.

Hectic pace over-stimulates as well. There is no need to hurry children from one activity to the next. Perhaps a child's most important learning today is mastering the zip on his coat – but if he is rushed, that learning is interrupted. There is always tomorrow to play that other game or make the next discovery.

Bright colour is highly stimulating. In the late 1900s there was a prevailing feeling that children should be continually surrounded by brilliant, primary colours. Walls, carpets, curtains and furniture were done in conflicting hues and patterns. Current trends reflect a growing understanding that children relax and focus better in a more tranquil environment; so in many nurseries today calm tints predominate, with the bright reverberating colours kept to specific areas that invite a higher excitement level, for instance a room for music and dance. It is a good topic for staff discussion and a useful tip to pass on to parents.

Reggio research maintains that 'a significant chromatic presence is provided by the children themselves ... The environment thus should not be saturated with colour but should be slightly "bare" so that the best balance is reached when the space is inhabited.' In nature, vast expanses such as oceans, moors and sky are varying shades of calm colours. Intense hues come in small accents or fleeting moments – a flower, a butterfly or a sunset. Following this train of thought, a Devon headteacher specified cream-coloured walls and wood furniture throughout her new school. She said this neutral backdrop 'lets *me* paint the picture!' The wood's varying shades are easy on the eyes and bring a sense of visual tranquillity. Brightness and character are provided through children's artwork and intriguing articles that highlight particular areas.

Environment supporting children's learning

An understanding of how children learn is the basis for creating an enabling environment for them. The Welsh Foundation Phase Framework states, 'Children learn through first-hand experiential activities with the serious business of "play" providing the vehicle.' For young children, play is the primary method of exploration and discovery. Play is also how children formulate thoughts and share ideas. Even those who speak different languages have remarkable ability to communicate through play.

Play is intrinsic to well-being. Froebel (1974) said, 'Play gives children joy, freedom, contentment and peace with the world.' Even children who have suffered hardship have a remarkable urge to play – we see this in the news from war zones every day.

Much play is symbolic, for instance when children act out stories and experiences during role play or small-world play and when they build block constructions to represent places or objects. Such symbolic play precedes more complex forms of representation such as written language; children must have rich opportunities to communicate ideas in concrete ways before advancing to abstract ways. Many practitioners have noticed that while most girls in the Foundation Stage are comfortable expressing ideas through drawing, mark-making (and eventually writing), boys often continue expressing ideas in three-dimensional ways for a longer period. The environment must provide for every type of representation.

As children weave narratives through their play, they demonstrate the link between play and literacy. They absorb countless maths and physics concepts too while shaping sand, pouring water or building with blocks. Perhaps the most important learning developed through play is children's confidence and social interaction.

Lev Vygotsky (1978) wrote: 'In play, a child is always above his average age, above his daily behaviour; in play, it is as though he were a head taller than himself.' When parents and practitioners realise that play is building a strong foundation across all areas of learning, they allow it generous time and space.

Since play is children's primary mode of learning and is at the heart of their ability to thrive, the environment's quality can actually be measured in terms of the play taking place. Staff can scan the room and monitor: 'How many children are playing?' and 'How deeply involved are they?' These spot-checks should be applied periodically because assessment of the environment is ongoing. If the children are not deeply involved, it is time for staff conversations about what might be the reasons and how the space might be re-arranged.

Activity areas

A simple way to support learning through play is to divide the room into activity areas. This continuous provision enables children to make smooth transitions in their own time and follow individual interests much as they would at home. If any area is infrequently used, the space can be reorganised. Creating a motivational environment is an ongoing process.

Just as staff consider the overall mood of the setting, they need to consider also what mood and stimulation level to encourage within each activity area. They might place a bedside lamp and floor cushions in the book area to engender a quiet cosy feeling, for example.

Some common activity areas are listed below; these will vary depending on each setting's philosophy and the children's ages. Some areas are occasionally combined because of space constraints.

Welcome area

This makes a strong statement about a setting's ethos so deserves careful planning. Whether in a lobby or within the room, the welcome area is the threshold between a child's two worlds. Considering that this is where child, parent and key person connect each day, it is the perfect spot for cultural displays and posters in relevant languages. Children need a place to keep personal belongings, and they feel more secure if they know exactly where their things are. If the welcome area is spacious enough, parents feel free to linger, make friends themselves and become involved in the setting.

Construction and small-world

These are often combined in one area, where children build miniature environments with blocks and act out scenarios using little figures and vehicles. This area needs maximum floor space plus generous storage, and it must be protected from through-traffic so that children's creations don't get bumped. If this activity borders role play, materials can be readily shared; large construction work frequently evolves into role play.

Block play involves the whole child: children use large and fine motor skills and develop hand/eye coordination; they cooperate with others, solve problems, make plans and work out ideas. They gain maths and physics concepts of weight, length, width, balance, symmetry, design, fractions, proportion, counting, adding, subtracting. There is a strong connection too between block play and literacy. Figures 6.1 and 6.2 show two examples of where block play achieves this.

At first children tend to use blocks as individual pieces. Next they start placing blocks in rows or stacks. Gradually the play becomes more complex: bridging, enclosing, making patterns and designs, and eventually creating elaborate structures. Pat Gura and other experts suggest keeping accessories to a minimum initially to prevent distraction. But once

Figure 6.1 A teacher told his Year 2 and 3 class a fairy-tale about a dragon and a princess. Later in the construction corner, several of the children spontaneously recreated the story. They built this fantastic dragon with spikes down its back and a curving tail. See the knights marching to meet their fate between its jaws!

children are at home with block play, other materials and accessories can be provided as children love to act out narratives with miniature people, animals and vehicles – and they enjoy decorating their constructions. Some children prefer 'drawing' with blocks, making designs flat on floor or table. Most enjoy playing together, but sometimes a child gets an idea that he or she wants to construct alone, and this needs to be accommodated too.

Frequently children like to develop a project over several days; ideally, constructions are left intact until they are ready to dismantle them. But if everything must be cleared away, it is important to first acknowledge children's efforts, perhaps by discussing a construction or taking a photo. One child celebrated his castle by dancing round it; then he didn't mind taking it apart.

Clearing-up can be as much fun as building. A child might use one long block as an earthmover to push other blocks toward the shelf. If staff use shape names (square, rectangle, cylinder, ramp, etc.) as blocks are sorted into place, children naturally pick up these terms.

It is helpful to include clipboards, paper, markers, pencils and tape measures in the construction area. Relevant books can be displayed here too.

Figure 6.2 This boy is also re-enacting a story. Julian's teacher had told a tale called 'Easter Bunny Wonderland', and Julian made some Easter Bunnies out of marshmallows (one on a pedestal on the right, one in the background – you can see it just below his face). Then he created this 'wonderland' for them. Notice that he has used all four types of blocks: the large hollow blocks, mini-hollow blocks, unit blocks, and mini-units. He has built an unusual pathway with quarter-circles. He has made a car park beneath his edifice. Notice too that he has built a 'fence' around himself and his construction; sometimes children love to play together, but this was a time when he needed to work out his idea on his own.

Role play

This area too should be spacious enough for children to act out a wide array of scenarios, fantasies and stories. Rich social interaction takes place during role play, and imagination flourishes. Children need long stretches of time in this area to develop their ideas. It is a good place to include a cosy nook where a child can retreat into his or her imaginary world.

A unit to store dressing-up clothes and accessories is essential. These need not be complicated or elaborate. With a few oddments – like old handbags and oversize shoes – and some fabric bits, a child can be anything from a fireman to a fairy queen.

Role-play furniture should be child-sized and versatile, so that bedroom or kitchen can be transformed into doctor's surgery, garden centre or whatever inspiration suggests. Arches, windows and mirrors enhance this area.

Plastic food limits imagination and is unnecessary. Open-ended materials such as corks, conkers, clothes pegs, lids and cloth scraps are far more useful as they become anything in the hands of a child. Storybooks can inspire role play, and writing materials should be included here as well so children can jot down phone messages, etc.

Book area

Ideally this is situated in the corner furthest from noise and bustle. Books should be displayed in such a way that favourites can be easily recognised. Rather than having an overwhelming supply of books on hand, it is better to retain a limited number in the room, kept in orderly fashion so that children learn to respect and care for them. If staff are tuned-in to children's interests, they will know when it is time to rotate stock.

Soft seating in this area encourages curling up with a book or a friend, and this homely quality is particularly important in settings where children spend long hours; they need quiet places to retreat into during a busy day. This area is an ideal place to create a comfy nook or den – children learn to love books when they are provided in a cosy attractive space.

Science and discovery

Since science is a process of investigation, this is an especially exciting part of the room. The science/discovery area is often combined with wet play, as children learn so much while experimenting with water. This area is where magnifying glasses, magnets, pulleys, funnels and similar intriguing tools are kept.

Some sort of nature display should be the heart of the science area, because young children are instinctively drawn to nature. Here children and adults discover fascinating wonders together. Some settings have ant or worm farms, and if staff are comfortable with pets, children enjoy caring for fish, guinea pigs or gerbils. One Children's Centre we have seen has a much-loved old dog – but it is usually found on a rug in the book corner!

Wet and messy area

Learning is profound in the wet and messy area, which should be near the sink and ideally includes a water table, a wet-sand table, and a dry-

Figure 6.3 A 'smorgasbord' of creative materials

sand table – because these materials are very different from each other and invite involvement. Natural materials like twigs, pebbles and seashells complement the buckets and shovels found here. If this area is near an exit, wet activities can be readily brought outdoors where children can be even freer in their play.

Malleables are often incorporated in a wet area or art area. Dough, clay and Plasticine are excellent for sensory investigation, and children use all kinds of tools (including recycled objects) as they shape their creations.

Art area

Also near the sink with tools and materials readily accessible, this area should offer a smorgasbord to whet creative appetites; recycled and natural materials make excellent additions to commercial art products.

Creative activity here builds children's confidence and self-esteem. It opens avenues of discovery – as when a child is thrilled to realise what happens when blue and yellow paint mix. Adults must always remember that 'the process is more important than the product'.

Workshop or design and technology

A proper workbench is best in this area where children construct with wood and recycled materials. Tools should be real and reliable, not imitations. The critical aspect here is that the workbench is well supervised and protected from traffic. (Some centres start children hammering golf tees into pumpkins before progressing to nails into wood.)

A Creative Unit supplied with tools plus wire, string, tape, rubber bands, dowels and other useful craft materials will empower children to pursue their plans. Staff members engage their own creativity whilst setting up this multi-purpose workshop which spurs independence and imagination.

In *Bringing the Froebel Approach to Your Early Years Practice*, Helen Tovey (2013) describes this workshop area as 'a very dynamic place that will change from day to day, even from hour to hour. Many children use the workshop area to make props for their play, for example watches, magic wands, mobile phones, superhero capes, head-bands, crowns, and so on.' While a young child enjoys playing with materials and exploring their sensory qualities, an older child will use them with clear purpose. For instance, a two year old might pick up a cardboard tube to roll across the floor, while a four year old might use it to make a pair of spectacles.

When children get such ideas, they have determination to persist and they learn a great deal in the process. This is what Froebel called self-activity, emphasising that children need to discover their own challenges and then solve them. Of course staff awareness is crucial, because sometimes a child can visualise an idea but encounter difficulties achieving it. An adult can support with suggestive questions.

Mark-making

The name of this area varies from one setting to another: mark-making, writing, literacy, office, graphics. It is often adjacent to the book corner and sometimes borders art so that materials can be shared. However, many nurseries decide not to include a specified literacy area – they simply provide writing materials in every activity area to encourage mark-making throughout the room. The same holds true for maths.

Crossover between activity areas shows that children are learning to think for themselves and make connections – for example when a child takes paper and pen from the mark-making area to the home corner to make a shopping list, or fetches string to make spaghetti. Attractive links such as arches and windows between activity areas encourage this natural crossover.

Occasionally a child may play exclusively in one part of the room. In one nursery, for example, a boy played only with blocks every day. To broaden his experience, the teacher brought other activities into the construction area. Soon he was using dressing-up things and tools in the course of his block play, and it wasn't long before he ventured to other areas of the setting. Another solution might be to allow him to play with blocks outside the construction area. The environment should support the individual child's needs and interests.

Boundaries and flexibility

Activity areas need boundaries to provide security for children's focused play. These boundaries need not be permanent and must not interfere with supervision. Where possible, free-standing shelves offer flexible boundaries between learning areas, service the activities undertaken there, and provide places for displaying children's work, for example, models.

When each area is bounded on three sides, children's activity is protected from the disruption of through-traffic. In several settings where children were thought to have behavioural problems – because they kept running through the room and would not calm down – practitioners were astonished at the transformation when they moved shelves at right angles to the walls to divide the space into areas: the room became peaceful as children settled into sustained meaningful activity.

If a room's set-up never changes, it becomes like wallpaper that no one notices anymore; but a fresh arrangement can revive interest.

Everyone needs change occasionally; schools and nurseries do well to invest in flexible solutions using high quality robust equipment to allow every new cohort of children to benefit from the same quality of provision as the first intake; and the space can be made to look fresh and new for the new group. Just as people need 'elbow room', a children's setting needs to be able to shift within its space – to breathe, move about and get comfortable. Flexibility is key. Children might even assist in the process of change, giving them a sense of agency.

In a flexible environment, staff will be prompted to change the furniture layout to allow for:

- changes in ages or numbers of children;

- inclusion of children with special needs;

- behavioural challenges;

- recapturing interest;

- new seasons or themes;

- introduction of a new service (e.g. after-school club or community services).

Through observation, staff will know when children need the stability of keeping the set-up the same and when they are ready for change. In an open-plan nursery with flexible dividers, children can even lead the decision as to when they move up to join an older group – because they observe what is happening in other parts of the nursery and recognise staff and children and want to belong to that group. This supports sibling relationships and facilitates smooth transitions. If staff are tuned-in to the children, it will be apparent when the younger ones are eager to join the others. Equally, when a child feels they want some of that security they used to have in the baby or toddler room, or just a cuddle with their old key person there, they can have it.

Storage and display

Storage is important. Play materials, art supplies, books, dressing-up gear, science equipment, 'good junk', clothing, artefacts ... any practitioner could add to the list of necessary props. Storage should be considered early during the design phase to ensure that decisions truly support children and staff in their use of the space. Good storage is safe, located at point of use, child-accessible, clear and understandable, and aesthetically pleasing (Greenman 1988).

Built-in cupboards have their place, particularly for long-term storage in a corridor or attic. However movable free-standing shelves are best within the room, placed to create boundaries between areas and service each activity. A variety of shelf types will serve different functions. Most shelves should provide accessibility at point of use, encouraging independence as children select and return materials themselves.

Display should be included in each activity area as well – in fact, display panels can help partition areas. Display celebrates children's efforts and encourages them to build on what they know – youngsters like to revisit former projects, and visual reminders help scaffold their learning. And of course children love to show their parents what they have made. Displays should be respectful of the effort that went in and the pride children have in their work.

Both vertical displays (of photos and artwork) and horizontal displays (models and artefacts) should be changed frequently, to remain relevant and interesting and to ensure every child's work is at some point on display. Children's independence and confidence are strengthened if they are allowed to help make and maintain displays themselves, and staff can help them articulate what they want to show through role-modelling.

Movement, surfaces and furniture

Of course children need lots of time outdoors each day for the lively action that is essential to emotional well-being and healthy physical development. The indoor environment too must allow for children's need to move. Movement is actually what enables children to sit still, as being still requires advanced muscle control. Sally Goddard Blythe (2005) writes, 'Those children who are unable to stay still are showing their balance and motor systems are not yet sufficiently mature to remain still for long periods of time.' The floor is the primary play surface, where children can adjust their posture, shift around and feel in control.

To gain maximum use of floor space, the number of chairs and tables should be kept to a minimum. Of course, some chairs will be necessary. They must be stable and allow children to have their feet flat on the floor so they are comfortable and have optimum control of their upper bodies. (Chairs with sides give extra support to the youngest.) Table height must correspond: a 20 cm differential from seat to table top is recommended. Any tables should have multiple uses and be lightweight and movable. Height-adjustable tables are best as they may be quickly raised in height for stand-up activities or altered for children of varying sizes. (To be able to adjust a table's angle may be helpful too; a slightly slanted surface can give fuller control to a child with special needs.) If a table's legs can be unscrewed, it is easily stored away.

All furniture should be child-sized and sturdy with rounded edges. Wooden furniture lends a natural impression and is friendly to the touch. Its varieties of pattern and grain offer opportunities for learning: 'Look, this was part of a tree!' And because of its neutral colour, natural wood furniture blends with almost any style – it looks 'right' in a converted barn or a modern glass building.

Babies and toddlers have somewhat different needs from older children. Their environment must be set up in accordance with a sure knowledge of their development.

Babies' senses are awake from the beginning. The sense of touch affects newborns as their mothers caress, cuddle and care for them. As babies gain control of their movements, they reach up to touch the face above them; they like to feel with their feet too. They need objects of various textures to explore.

The sense of sight is active as a newborn studies his or her parents' faces and looks into their eyes. Pictures or contrasting patterns can provide visual stimulation, and babies love to watch movement so enjoy mobiles. If a cot or pram is placed beneath a tree, the infant will contentedly watch the interplay of light and shadow through moving leaves.

Birdsong and classical music are soothing for babies, but best of all is the human voice; a baby loves to listen to a familiar voice speak, croon or sing. It is exciting when babies discover their own voices and start making purposeful sounds. They also learn to make sounds by shaking or banging objects.

Young children experiment with taste as they try new foods and explore objects with gums and tongue. Margaret McMillan planted borders of roses, lavender and herbs so children could have pleasant experiences of smell too.

Because babies learn through all their senses, their environment must provide suitable opportunities and materials. Many nurseries use treasure baskets filled with everyday items of varying tactile qualities for babies to scrutinise, squeeze, rub, bang, shake, and mouth at leisure: whisk, measuring spoons, bottle brush, lemon, fir cone, sponge, leather glove, sea shell, wooden spoon. Practitioners maintain safety and cleanliness as well as adding new objects to keep the babies' interest.

In *People Under Three* (1994), Elinor Goldschmied and Sonia Jackson introduced *heuristic* play. ('Heuristic' means helping to find out or discover and has the same root as *eureka*.) Heuristic play was conceived with one and two year olds in mind, offering an opportunity to experiment with a wide range of objects in a treasure basket.

> Children have a natural curiosity to investigate, so by providing items such as tins, corks, lids, cardboard tubes, chains and clothes pegs, we are supporting this exploration. Whilst the heuristic play session is in process, adults need to remain seated and quiet. This supports children in making their own choices and discoveries.
>
> (Crowther 2012)

Children of this age love to sort or arrange objects and *do* things with them, so it is essential to provide large quantities of each item.

Regarding babies' physicality, they develop with amazing rapidity: from helpless newborns to confident crawlers or novice walkers in one year. They have an inborn drive to continually stretch their abilities, so the whole environment must support their urge to interact with everything around them. It is important for the youngest to be on surfaces where they can master new skills such as rolling over, reaching, and eventually finding their own methods of inching forward. From about three months, they are able to spend some time on the floor in a protected area with their key person beside them.

When babies learn to sit, they can suddenly observe much that was previously invisible to them. This is exciting but can also be frustrating, as an infant notices objects and activities that are out of reach. This is one reason the treasure basket is such an asset, offering exploration in spite of the child's lack of mobility.

As babies learn to move and crawl, they want to get going. Crawlers and toddlers enjoy climbing, sliding, crawling through a barrel . . . They learn through repetition and practice every new action over and over.

Prior to walking independently, children learn to pull to a stand and then 'cruise', grasping anything in reach for support. It is important that furniture is stable, offers handholds and has rounded edges. Playthings that encourage balance and practice in walking are helpful at this stage, for example a pushcart, a sturdy chair or even a strong cardboard box to push.

Because their experience centres around sensory exploration and physical movement, the following activity areas are recommended for under-threes:

- *Active play area* with maximum floor space and a nursery gym or similar structure on which children develop their spatial awareness, physicality, sense of balance – and feelings of confidence and well-being. A small amount of furniture to support emergent role play, small-world play and block play complements this area too.

- *Wet area* located near the sink including malleables and sand for sensory exploration, as well as floor easels and basic art supplies. The wet area can double as a mealtime area.

- *Safe crawl area*, contained and cosy for non-mobile babies. This is the perfect place to include a little sensory corner with mirrors, CDs, crackly cellophane, rubber, emery paper, etc. on the walls and sheepskin and treasure basket on the floor.

- *Quiet area* where children can relax and sleep or spend cosy time with their key person and books. A glider (a kind of rocking chair that moves back and forth on a gliding mechanism) is lovely here to support bonding.

Conclusion

Finally, adults setting up the environment must get down on the children's level and consider: if I were a child, how would I feel in this place? Am I warm enough on the floor? Do the spaces welcome me in and lead me on? Are there areas that offer the thrill of adventure to support my big moments and cosy nooks for when I'm feeling small? And even more important than this environment: are there adults who love and understand me? Will I be accepted and happy here?

An empowering environment allows children to take the initiative, explore all possibilities and grasp the potential for play and discovery. They can construct and imagine, make decisions and learn to think for themselves. Such a space is beautiful, peaceful – and intriguing. It stimulates curiosity, creativity, confidence and cooperation. It invites children to enter and helps them feel at home. The environment becomes a friend to the children and the adults' best assistant.

References and further reading

Bradburn, E. (1989) *Margaret McMillan, Portrait of a Pioneer*. London: Routledge.

Ceppi, G. and Zini, M. (eds) (1998) *Children, Spaces, Relations*. Reggio Domus Research.

Community Playthings (2005) *Foundations: The Value of Block Play* (DVD).

Community Playthings (2008) *I Made a Unicorn.*

Community Playthings (2012) *What Happens in the Baby Room?*

Community Playthings (2012) *Spaces – Room Layout for 0–5 Year Olds.*

Community Playthings (2013) *A Good Place to Be Two.*

Community Playthings (2014) *The Irresistible Classroom – Getting the Learning Environment Right in Reception and Key Stage 1.*

Crowther, C. (2012) Atelier Nursery, Bath. Interview, April 2012.

DfE (2011) *Statutory Framework for the Early Years Foundation: Setting the Standards for Learning, Development and Care for Children from Birth to Five: Stage Draft for Consultation.* Web-based publication downloaded from DoE website.

DfES (2002) *Birth to Three Matters: A Framework to Support Children in their Earliest Years.* London: DfES Publications.

DfES (2004) *Building for Sure Start: A Design Guide.* London: DfES Publications.

DfES (2007) *The Early Years Foundation Stage: Setting the Standards for Learning, Development and Care for Children from Birth to Five.* Nottingham: DfES Publications.

Edgington, M. (1999) *The Nursery Teacher in Action*, 2nd edn. London: Paul Chapman Publishing.

Edwards, C. *et al.* (1998) *The Hundred Languages of Children: The Reggio Emilia Approach to Early Childhood Education.* London: Ablex Publishing Corporation.

Fisher, J. (2010) *Moving on to Key Stage 1: Improving Transition from the Early Years Foundation Stage.* Maidenhead: Open University Press.

Froebel, F. (1974) *The Education of Man.* Clifton, NJ: A.M. Kelly reprint.

Goddard Blythe, S. (2005) *The Well Balanced Child: Movement and Early Learning.* Stroud: Hawthorn Press.

Goldschmied, E. and Jackson, S. (1994) *People Under Three: Young Children in Day Care* (2nd edn, 2004; 3rd edn, 2015). London: Routledge.

Greenman, J. (1988) *Caring Spaces, Learning Places.* Redmond, WA: Exchange Press.

Gura, P. (ed.), with the Froebel Block Play Research Group directed by Tina Bruce (1992) *Exploring Learning: Young Children and Block Play.* London: Paul Chapman Publishing.

Hohmann, M. and Weikart, D. (eds) (1995) *Educating Young Children.* Ypsilanti, MI: High/Scope Press.

Olds, A. (2000) *Child Care Design Guide.* New York: McGraw-Hill.

Pardee, M. (2005) *Community Investment Collaborative for Kids Resource Guide.* New York: Local Initiatives Support Corporation.

Tovey, H. (2013) *Bringing the Froebel Approach to Your Early Years Practice.* London: Routledge.

Vygotsky, L. (1978) *Mind in Society.* Cambridge, MA: Harvard University Press.

Welsh Assembly Government (2008) *Foundation Phase Framework for Children's Learning 3–7 Years.* Cardiff: Welsh Assembly Government.

Researching the benefits of the outdoor environment for children

Ian Frampton, Rebecca Jenkin and Philip Waters

Context

The European Centre for Environment and Human Health (ECEHH), based in Truro, in Cornwall, is a part of the University of Exeter Medical School. It is part-funded by the European Social Fund through the EU Convergence Programme, which supports research related to the knowledge economy, labour market and human capital linked to employment and skills needs now and in the future, including activities that support training of researchers and postgraduate studies. The aim of ECEHH is to explore the links between our environment and our health, including both health risks and benefits. Previous research has focused on the health *risks* inherent in the environment (associated with climate change, pollution and other man-made dangers such as road traffic); we know a lot less about the potential health *benefits* of the natural environment, especially for children.

Graduate and post-doctoral researchers based at ECEHH have developed a range of research themes to explore the potential benefits of the natural environment for human health (see www.ecehh.org for details on our latest projects). Some of the striking findings from this work – such as the discovery that living within two kilometres of the coast confers a significant benefit on positive mental health and well-being in adults (White *et al.* 2013) – may also hold for children, and studies are ongoing. In addition, we have also developed a research theme specifically to investigate the health and well-being benefits of the outdoor environment for children, especially for play and for learning. Some of our work is focused on school-aged children (partly because they make more biddable research participants), and so in reviewing these studies we may need to 'extrapolate backwards in time' to reflect on the potential implications for early years settings. We have also developed new research methods to help us explore the experience of younger children directly – and some of these are presented for the first time in this chapter. We gratefully acknowledge the support and contribution of our colleagues in the Cornwall Children's Outdoor Play Forum, who have helped to develop and shape the ideas presented here.

Introduction

The natural environment is a vital space for children's learning. Freedom to move through space enables children to discover spatial relationships, which in turn are fundamental building blocks of higher-level thinking skills. Exploring and developing physical skills such as balance and movement has a direct positive effect on well-being and self-esteem. The outdoor environment can also be a powerful place for children to explore their creativity. However, the perceived risks of the outdoors and adult over-estimation of harm have seriously curtailed young children's freedom to explore their outdoor world. This chapter draws on the latest research findings to redress this imbalance and to offer nursery managers and practitioners powerful arguments to use in support of the value and vital importance of outdoor play and learning space for young children.

Connection with nature and the outdoor world

By engaging with the outdoor environment, young children significantly increase their 'nature connectedness', which in turn has a positive effect on their well-being and long-term interest in the world around them. This section reviews the latest evidence for children's preference for the outdoors and the benefits of encouraging children to view themselves as 'custodians' of the future of the natural environment.

Early childhood experiences in nature significantly increase the likelihood that children will develop lifelong positive attitudes towards the environment and environmental issues (Chawla 2009). Furthermore, it is hypothesised that regular contact with nature during childhood can lead to positive ecological attitudes and behaviours in adulthood (Waite 2007). The environmental conditions a child becomes accustomed to in early life serve as a benchmark against which they will measure environmental degradation in their future (Kahn 2001); reduced experience of natural environments in childhood risks ignorance toward declining environmental conditions (Gilbertson 2012).

Children who grow up with access to safe outdoor play space also develop a greater sense of connection with their community; and communities that enhance social capital by securing safe outdoor play spaces raise happier children. Not everyone can live in a safe rural environment, yet it is possible that community-level action by groups of concerned adults, including early years specialists, can make a huge difference in a range or urban, city and rural contexts.

The powerful concept of 'Nature-Deficit Disorder' was introduced by Louv (2005) in an influential book entitled *Last Child in the Woods*. Louv explored how human beings, especially children, are spending less time outdoors, and how this could be contributing to a wide range of behavioural problems. Part of our work in ECEHH is to explore how children experience different environments and to identify the potential health and developmental benefits.

Research Study 1: Identifying children's play preferences

At ECEHH we have been working together with a local community interest company, Exhale (www.exhale.org.uk), to explore how children value the outdoor environment as a play space. Exhale was commissioned by the local NHS primary care trust to deliver evidence-based family-level interventions for children who are clinically overweight or obese. Exhale developed an award-winning programme called 'Keep It In The Family' (KIITF; NICE 2012), based on an existing evidence-based intervention called 'MEND' (Mind, Education, Nutrition, Do it!), initially developed by the Institute of Child Health, University of London (www.mendcentral.org). The KIITF programme is designed specifically to meet the needs of 'hard to reach' families who need a more intensive intervention, including an individualised approach and flexible support over a longer time period than MEND can offer. Such families are 'hardly reached' by conventional interventions, are under-represented in practice, and more likely to drop out of treatment (Davis *et al.* 2012).

The original MEND programme offers a suite of evidence-based interventions to help parents and children live fitter, healthier and happier lives, including a programme designed specifically for preschool children aged two to four. One of the benefits of MEND is that it is designed to be delivered in urban settings that do not have access to safe outdoor play space. The programme can be located in sports halls and other indoor venues, which is one of its great strengths. However, Exhale were interested to explore whether there would be additional benefits in delivery in a rural, coastal context in north Cornwall.

Exhale therefore developed KIITF as a two-stage programme. In the first stage, families are referred by GPs and other primary healthcare providers in the context of at least one child in the family being significantly overweight. The families participate in a conventional ten-week MEND programme delivered in a local community setting, such as a school or sports centre. At the end of this stage of the programme, families are invited to participate in a follow-on MEND-plus programme. This additional ten-week programme offers families the opportunity to try out a range of activities using local facilities, including beach and coastal activities such as surfing and coasteering that are available in the local environment.

For the purposes of this study, we were interested in how children would rate the acceptability of different activities, both indoor and outdoor. Typically, the 'acceptability' of these sorts of interventions is determined by how many families complete the overall intervention (on the basis that the lower the dropout, the more acceptable it is). Alternatively, some projects collect 'customer satisfaction' data at the end of the intervention to identify what the participants liked doing best. Our aim for this study was to develop a new method to give children the opportunity to provide feedback on their experience of different types of activities more directly. This feedback is important in studies aiming to explore the relationship between acceptability and outcome, especially for novel interventions. In the adult literature, a diary-based approach called the Day Reconstruction Method (DRM: White and Dolan 2009) has been used to explore how much pleasure participants get from an activity and how rewarding they experienced it to be. For example, chores such as housework may not be experienced as very pleasurable, but the outcome of a tidy house could be rewarding.

These concepts may be difficult for younger children to grasp, especially if we are asking them to recall events based on diary keeping. We have therefore developed a simplified version of the DRM scale that distinguishes between thoughts (e.g. 'I'm good at this activity') and feelings (e.g. 'I felt happy when I did this activity'). Using this approach, we first reminded children of the range of activities in their day using visual prompts presented on an iPad.

For each activity, we asked children to respond to questions, generating a Feelings Score and a Thoughts Score. Figure 7.1 shows that children are able to define clear differences in both these dimensions between different activities. It is noteworthy that being outside, with friends and with family, at the beach and engaging in KIITF activities are rated higher than video gaming, TV or – perhaps more obviously – school. Further work on this measure, to explore its psychometric properties and to develop versions for use with younger children, is ongoing.

The risk/benefit equation

> [risky] play is vital for a child's development and should not be sacrificed to the cause of overzealous and disproportionate risk assessments.
>
> (Young 2010)

Too much emphasis in recent years has been placed on the potential risks and liabilities associated with outdoor play space for young children. Fortunately, recent research is helping to shift policy makers to a more balanced view, highlighting the benefits of outdoor environments and the risks of *not* giving children access to outdoor play space. This section reviews the latest evidence and shares some inspirational outdoor play space design.

The value of 'risky play' as a vital component of outdoor play for preschool children has been well established (Sandseter 2009a, 2009b). However, play equipment manufacturers have identified that perceived risk of potential for accidents, and perceived legal liability issues, are significant inhibitory factors in preventing parish councils and other local community organisations from supporting plans to develop outdoor play facilities. In our local context in Cornwall, we have been working together with Taylor Design and Play (www.taylordesignandplay.com) and the Law School at the University of Exeter to explore the legal context for outdoor play space, including early years settings.

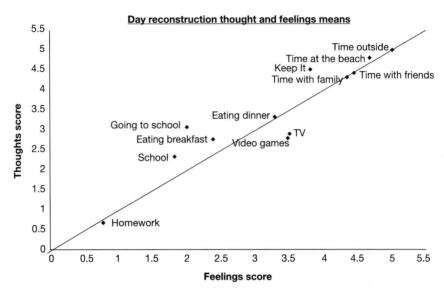

Figure 7.1 Average Feelings and Thoughts scores for KIITF and daily activities

From a legal perspective several elements of law intersect in relation to the 'active' world, intersections which become particularly sensitive where children are involved: the 'common law' principles of negligence in tort and contract liability are added to with a range of statutory sources and guidelines, domestic and European. For early years settings, Health and Safety Executive guidance is also relevant, including the Health and Safety at Work Act 1974, along with the Reporting of Injuries, Diseases and Dangerous Occurrences Regulations 1985. Additional relevant sources include the Control of Substances Hazardous to Health Regulations 1994, the Workplace (Health, Safety and Welfare) Regulations 1992, the Occupiers' Liability Acts of 1957 and 1984, the Activity Centre (Young Persons' Safety) Act 1985 as set out in the Adventure Activities Licensing Regulations 1996 and, in relation to the design and construction of play materials, the European Standards for Playground Equipment, BS EN 1176 and 1177.

In October 2010, Lord Young published his report *Common Sense, Common Safety*. The report puts forward a series of policies for improving the perception of health and safety, to ensure it is taken seriously by employers and the general public, while ensuring the burden on small businesses (including early years settings) is minimised. The report also promises that health and safety laws will be reviewed to ensure that the rules for workplaces (the original remit of the Health and

Safety Executive) are separated from play and leisure settings including early years.

There is growing recognition of the obstacles to healthy development presented by over-defensive responses to perceived legal threats and the resultant implementation of risk-averse rather than risk-reducing policies. Recent case law (Harris v Perry and another [2008] EWCA Civ 907, Poppleton v Portsmouth Youth Activities Committee (2008) EWCA Civ 646, and R v Porter [2008] EWCA Crim 1271) demonstrates a range of potential issues that may arise in relation to injury resulting from activity.

Fortunately, the Appeal Court reversals in all these cases also demonstrate a willingness on the part of the courts to minimise the growth of litigation that would prioritise safety over activity. Nevertheless, businesses involved in producing play equipment and resources, as well as businesses (which in this context includes early years settings) and public authority organisations involved in managing them, must negotiate this complex field of law and the changing philosophy which underpins it.

From a legal perspective for early years settings, the provision of physically varied and demanding exercise contexts is important not only in relation to the maintenance of healthy weight but also in providing opportunities for children to learn how their bodies 'work' in space, building muscle tone and brain responses and so reducing the likelihood of accidental injury should they encounter less controlled environments as they grow (Professor Melanie Williams, personal communication). Authorities, institutions and providers of commercial sports and play equipment must of course remain alert to the safety implications of their products and practices and to the reasonable guidance provided by legislative supporting sources.

A general principle of law is sometimes acknowledged to the effect that contributory negligence is unlikely to be attributed to children (but see for example a recent attribution of 50 per cent contributory negligence in a case in Scotland in relation to a nine year old child – Lisa Wardle v Scottish Borders Council (PD13/08) Sheriff Principal, 31 January 2011, 2011 WL 722358). Nevertheless, consideration of the balance between appropriate protection of children and *unnecessarily risk-averse* policies in early years settings could be a valuable contribution to policy development and practice.

We have been very fortunate at ECEHH in being able to host workshops for local early years providers with PLAYLINK (www.playlink.org) to explore how a more enlightened approach to risk-benefit analysis could revolutionise the promotion of beneficial risk-taking in play. PLAYLINK is a multi-disciplinary group working to improve people's – children's, teenagers', adults' – experience and enjoyment of the outdoors. PLAYLINK works across a variety of settings: the general public realm, parks, social and mixed tenure housing, and specialist provision such as schools and Children's Centres.

A wonderful example of this approach is demonstrated by Lark Hill Nursery School in Stockport, with their Muddy Slide. Young children are encouraged by the nursery staff to pour muddy water down the slide to make it faster – with hilarious consequences (see www.youtube.com/embed/4JUAFqvmOGk). Staff are on hand at all times to ensure the safety of the children; though they remain in the background, consistently offering positive and enabling comments to support the children's play. As noted on the PLAYLINK website, the result is 'simply a delight and an expression of common sense judgment by the staff'.

Nutrition, health and exercise

> Historically, a fat child meant a healthy child, one who was likely to survive the rigors of undernourishment and infection. In the past decade, however, excessive fatness has arguably become the primary childhood health problem in developed nations.
>
> (Ebbeling *et al.* 2002: 473)

In the last decade, the scale of the public health crisis of childhood obesity has continued to grow. The current and future burden to UK society of childhood obesity was explored by a Foresight review (UK Government Office for Science 2007). The review predicted an increase in prevalence such that by 2050 55 per cent of boys and 70 per cent of girls in the UK could be overweight or obese. Outdoor play space is a vital factor in helping children to maintain a positive energy balance and to develop lifelong skills and habits. Recent research from our centre and elsewhere shows how access to the outdoor environment in the early years has a profoundly positive effect on long-term physical health and well-being.

Research Study 2: Narrative journeys in the grounds of a preschool

In the context of increasing obesity and reduced activity levels, it is encouraging that a recent report adopted by the majority of MEPs and reported in the European Law Monitor (www.europeanlawmonitor.org/Latest-EU-News/physical-education-should-be-compulsory-in-schools.html) advocates compulsory physical education (PE) lessons in schools to increase children's activity levels. However, school-based sports and physical education approaches are not suited to all children, especially those who are not naturally drawn to skill-based team games. Despite attempts to increase PE in schools, international research indicates that formal PE may actually discourage some young children from adopting lifelong interests in physical activity (Burdette and Whitaker 2005; Dobbins *et al.* 2009).

This is in stark contrast to the literature which suggests that when left to their own devices children's play is often very physically active (Staempfli 2009). At ECEHH we have been evaluating a novel approach to encouraging children (and adults) to become more active and to explore their outdoor environment through a technique called Narrative Journey (Waters 2011), rather than through traditional sporting activities. The basic premise is that a narrative or story is constructed and delivered as cues that invite players on a journey through a landscape. A cue could be as simple as highlighting indentations in mud and claiming them to be the footprints of extinct or even mythical beings; the ambition being that children will be excited by the possibility and play out experiences that are connected to exploration at ground level, where they might then happen upon all sorts of play affordances and materials. Narrative Journey could equally be an epic adventure or quest planted within a landscape inviting players to embark on a day-long (or longer) journey. Narrative Journey can be used as a training tool, where learning concepts are written into an unfolding story (Waters 2014; Waters *et al.* 2014).

Although Narrative Journey draws on practices from across allied fields (Playwork, Place-Based Education and Performative Storytelling), it combines these in new ways that have not yet been applied in formal settings like schools. In the context of early years practice, for example, there is a conflict between play being understood for its inherent qualities, and therefore not to be shaped, manipulated or structured by adults (Elkind 2007), as opposed to play being used instrumentally as a vehicle for formal learning (e.g. Bairaktarova *et al.* 2011). Narrative Journey aims to provide an intervention that can be adopted by practitioners from either of those stances by reframing practice as playful, and through positioning practitioners as players within children's experience, rather than as observers or adjudicators on the outside.

Our Narrative Journey research project is located in the Zelda School (www.zeldaschool.co.uk), a small Steiner-orientated nursery and infant school in Cornwall. This setting was selected as an optimum environment for researching children's outdoor nature experiences and for developing Narrative Journey praxis due to the long periods outdoors that children enjoy. The school has twenty-eight children aged between three and eight years; five of whom are being intensively tracked as a case series for our research project.

One of the main challenges in researching young children's outdoor play is that as adult observers we influence what happens in a play space simply by being there. From an anthropological perspective, we cannot help but influence the environment as participant-observers. To overcome this issue the project uses Behaviour Mapping (Cosco *et al.* 2010): a method where children are tracked with a camera as they move about an environment, with the resultant behaviour being coded using a specialised coding software that brings together behavioural and contextual data.

In this project, a multi-camera approach is being used, including the addition of cameras worn by participants that provide insights into children's direct experiences not normally observed in traditional ethnographic research. This method in particular is aligned with child-friendly participatory research methods because it locates children's direct experiences within the heart of the research. In addition, dialogic mapping is used to record and code children's monologues and dialogues; and map these onto the environmental contextual data to provide a far richer content for analysis. The use of video cameras also enables us to closely 'map' the movements of children through the landscape at a higher resolution than is possible using alternative methods such as wrist-mounted GPS devices.

Although it is too early in the research to draw any formal conclusions, there are some indicators that children in this study have a broader range of physical activities when their play has a narrative theme; an emerging story. This could suggest that children rarely engage in locomotor play just for the enjoyment of the physical activity itself, but instead it might be the emerging story that necessitates it – for example being chased by trolls or climbing under bushes to seek out fairies.

For early years practitioners this knowledge could add a valuable contribution to the design of alternative physical activity experiences, which could motivate children to be active because they enjoy the context for their movements, rather than movement that is narrowly defined or framed by a particular sport. We are developing a Narrative Journey manual to help practitioners develop story-based approaches in early years settings; for more details of this ongoing research theme, visit www.ecehh.org.

The outdoor environment and developing skills for learning

One of the research themes in ECEHH has been to explore how outdoor environments help to develop children's self-control and attention abilities, which are vital components of learning across early years and beyond. It has been hypothesised that attention is a finite cognitive resource that can be restored in specific ways once it has been depleted – the so-called Attention Restoration Theory (ART; Kaplan 1995). ART proposes that natural environments play a crucial role in restoring attentional capacity by invoking *involuntary* attention, and thus allowing *directed* attention to recover from fatigue.

In a previous study by Faber-Taylor and Kuo (2009), children between the ages of seven and twelve who had been clinically diagnosed with an Attention Deficit Disorder (ADD) took a walk through a city park and two urban environments (a downtown area and a residential area). After each walk the children's attention was assessed using a standardised measure of concentration used in diagnosing ADD. The results of the study indicated that children performed better on this test when they had been for a walk in the city park, compared to when they had walked through either the downtown or the residential (urban) areas. This indicates that the 'green' environment of the park enabled the children to concentrate better on a subsequent attention task. However, it is unclear whether the same effect would hold for children who have not been clinically diagnosed with ADD.

Research Study 3: Natural environments, self-control, attention and learning

We have therefore been conducting a series of 'laboratory' experiments in collaboration with local primary schools to explore how exposure to urban and natural environments influences children's attention and self-control abilities. For some of our studies, children have watched video clips of city, rural or 'control' (screensaver animations) environments, and in other studies children are taken on a short walk through a built or natural environment. Each time their attention and self-control were assessed before and afterwards. Analyses of these data are ongoing (see www.ecehh.org); however, at this early stage we are finding some very interesting results. Preliminary analyses suggest that as well as natural environments *restoring* attention and self-control, it appears that exposure to urban man-made environments is *decreasing* self-control capabilities (see Figure 7.2). We are now exploring whether exposure to natural environments can subsequently *recover* attention and self-control capabilities that have been depleted in urban environments; these findings will have important implications for access to natural environments, especially for children in urban early years settings and for urban planning for children more generally.

These sorts of research studies are difficult to conduct with preschool children, as we rely on the participants' ability to complete complex assessments of attention and self-control that are not readily available for younger children. Although we are able to 'extrapolate backwards' from our findings in older children, alternative research strategies could adopt a longitudinal approach to explore the long-term educational outcomes for children raised in different early years settings.

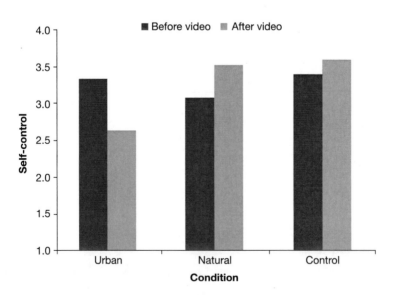

Figure 7.2 Children viewing the urban video scene scored significantly worse on a self-control measure in the post-test compared to their pre-test; children viewing the natural video scene scored significantly better.

We are also beginning to develop more direct ways of investigating the way the brain responds to different types of environment using functional brain imaging techniques. These sorts of brain scans are safe – there is no radiation involved – and relatively quick to conduct, so they can potentially be used with young children. At our collaborating imaging centre at King's College London, young children are prepared for the noisy and 'alien' scanner environment by practising in a fully-functioning mock scanner that has been set up like a spaceship. Getting used to being in the scanner as a mini-astronaut has proven to be an effective strategy to make sure that young children enjoy the whole experience.

Our initial work to date has been conducted using undergraduate participants, chiefly radiography students who benefit from finding out what it feels like to be in the scanner. Preliminary findings from this work show striking differences in brain activation in response to still images of urban versus rural environments, including in emotion processing networks, suggesting that our response to outdoor environments may be driven by profound neurobiological mechanisms that recognise the natural world as a familiar and safe place (Venkatasubramanian *et al.* 2013). By extending this research to young children in the future, we will be able to explore the extent to which these responses are innate or learned.

Early years settings and the outdoor environment: investment for long life

Historically, public health approaches have focused on the risks associated with the outdoor environment, such as pollution, infection and accidents. Yet from an educational perspective, writers from Rousseau (1783) onwards have understood the benefits of the natural environment as a setting for learning. Rousseau's hypothetical boy, Émile, is to be raised in the countryside, which he believed to be a more natural and healthy environment than the city. It is intuitively compelling that the natural environment *should* confer significant benefits for young children's health and well-being. However, it is only fairly recently that research has begun systematically to explore these issues.

At ECEHH, we have focused on investigating the potential benefits of the outdoor environment for young children's play, health and learning. Our findings to date suggest that children prefer activities in natural environments, which in turn may confer an advantage in tackling obesity by increasing activity levels. The outdoor environment is an attractive place for families (Ashbullby *et al.* 2013), offering a space to be together even for those families that are 'hardly reached' by conventional services.

Alternative approaches to formal physical education using storytelling appear to be effective in early years settings in promoting playful activity. Our experimental studies with school-aged children suggest that as well as natural environments *restoring* attention and self-control, exposure to urban man-made environments is *decreasing* self-control capabilities, with important implications for urban planning for children. Novel experimental approaches such as functional brain imaging may be helpful in characterising the innate response of young children to the outdoor world.

Recent preoccupation with potential risks associated with outdoor play (or more generally with the outdoor environment *per se*) has contributed to a risk-averse culture of anticipating hypothetical dangers at the expense of the potential benefits; though our understanding of the *benefits of risk* is starting to address the imbalance. Early years settings have been pivotal and brave in resisting the trend toward 'editing out' any risk from the child's world. In all the ways identified in this chapter, early years provision has a vital role to play in supporting policy makers, parents and ultimately children themselves to maximise the multiple benefits conferred by the natural world around them.

References

Ashbullby, K.J., Pahl, S., Webley, P. and White, M. (2013) The beach as a setting for families' health promotion: a qualitative study with parents and children living in coastal regions in Southwest England. *Health and Place* 23, 138–147.

Bairaktarova, D., Evangelou, D., Bagiati, A. and Brophy, S. (2011) Early engineering in young children's exploratory play with tangible materials. *Children, Youth and Environments* 21, 24.

Burdette, H.L. and Whitaker, R.C. (2005) Resurrecting free play in young children: looking beyond fitness and fatness to attention, affiliation, and affect. *Archives of Pediatrics and Adolescent Medicine* 159(1), 46–50.

Chawla, L. (2009) Growing up green: becoming an agent of care for the natural world. *Journal of Developmental Processes* 4, 6–23.

Cosco, N.G., Moore, R.C. and Islam, M.Z. (2010) Behaviour Mapping: a method for linking preschool physical activity and outdoor design. *Medicine and Science in Sports and Exercise* 42, 7.

Davis, F., McDonald, L. and Axford, N. (2012) *Technique Is Not Enough: A Framework for Ensuring that Evidence-Based Parenting Programmes Are Socially Inclusive.* Leicester: British Psychological Society.

Dobbins, M., De Corby, K., Robeson, P., Husson, H. and Tirilis, D. (2009) School-based physical activity programs for promoting physical activity and fitness in children and adolescents aged 6–18. *Cochrane Database of Systematic Reviews*, January(1), CD007651.

Ebbeling, C.B., Pawlak, D.B. and Ludwig, D.S. (2002) Childhood obesity: public-health crisis, common sense cure. *Lancet* 360(9331), 473–482.

Elkind, D. (2007) *The Power of Play: How Spontaneous, Imaginative Activities Lead to Happier, Healthier Children.* Cambridge, MA: Da Capo Press.

Faber-Taylor, A. and Kuo, F.E. (2009) Children with attention deficits concentrate better after walk in the park. *Journal of Attention Disorders* 12, 402–409.

Gilbertson, E. (2012) When nature speaks: evoking connectedness with nature in children through role-play in outdoor programming. MA thesis, University of Alberta.

Kahn, P.H. (2001) Structural-developmental theory and children's experience of nature. Paper presented at the Biennial Meeting of the Society for Research in Child Development, Minneapolis, MN, ERIC Document Reproduction Service.

Kaplan, S. (1995) The restorative benefits of nature: towards an integrative framework. *Journal of Environmental Psychology* 15, 169–182.

Louv, R. (2005) *Last Child in the Woods: Saving Our Children from Nature-Deficit Disorder.* Chapel Hill, NC: Algonquin Books.

NICE (2012) Tackling obesity in a rural county – a work in progress: obesity – working with local communities. *Public Health Guidance 42: Expert Case Study 15.*

Rousseau, J.J. (1783) *Émile, ou De l'éducation.* London: H. Baldwin.

Sandseter, E.B.H. (2009a) Affordances for risky play in preschool: the importance of features in the play environment. *Early Childhood Education* 36, 439–466.

Sandseter, E.B.H. (2009b) Children's expressions of exhilaration and fear in risky play. *Contemporary Issues in Early Childhood* 10, 92–106.

Staempfli, M.B. (2009) Reintroducing adventure into children's outdoor play environments. *Environment and Behavior* 41, 268–280.

UK Government Office for Science (2007) *Reducing Obesity: Future Choices*. London: HMSO.

Venkatasubramanian, S., Frampton, I., White, M., Fulford, J., Rock, B., Reville, M.-C., Hignett, A. and Depledge, M. (2013) Neural activation differences between water and non-water environments. Poster presented at the Environment and Human Health Forum, Truro, 13 September.

Waite, S. (2007) 'Memories are made of this': some reflections on outdoor learning and recall. *Education 3–13* 35, 333–347.

Waters, P. (2011) Trees talk: are you listening? Nature, narrative and children's anthropocentric place-based play. *Children, Youth and Environments* 21(1), 10.

Waters, P. (2014) Into the woods: stories and nature in playwork training. *Children, Youth and Environments*, in press.

Waters, P., Waite, S. and Frampton, I. (2014) Play frames, or framed play? The use of film cameras in visual ethnographic research with children. *International Journal of Playwork*, 1(1), 23–38.

White, M.P. and Dolan, P. (2009) Accounting for the richness of daily activities. *Psychological Science* 20, 1000–1008.

White, M.P., Alcock, I., Wheeler, B.W. and Depledge, M.H. (2013) Coastal proximity, health and well-being: results from a longitudinal panel survey. *Health & Place*, 23, 97–103.

Young, Lord (2010) *Common Sense, Common Safety*. London: HM Government.

CHAPTER 8

Research into practice

Susan Hay

The contributors to this book have done exactly what I had hoped for, and shown us that much of what many believed to be true *is* true in relation to the way children thrive as young children and later as school children. A number of common threads are woven through the chapters from the various perspectives of the contributors, and this end piece simply attempts to highlight them, and add a few more references to explore later.

Children's 'wiring'

We have learned a great deal from early brain development research in the last few years; however in Chapter 1, Professor Philip Gammage reminds us that it is sometimes difficult to relate this to practice, and that brain research yields 'rough indicators' only for designing how young children learn and our aspiration should be to reach 'optimal conditions' for learning. It is most important at this stage to be aware of the debate, and what findings we should watch out for in the future which are translational. The facts we know have been summarised by Pam Schiller (2010) in the US-based *Exchange*, and can help prompt us to think about the windows of opportunity we have to influence and support children's learning:

- The brain of a three year old is 2.5 times more active than an adult's.

- Brain development is contingent on a complex interplay between genes and the environment.

- Experience 'wires' the brain, and repetition strengthens the wiring.

- Brain development is non-linear.

- Early relationships affect wiring.

We know that the 'wiring' referred to – the making of connections – is through contact, observations, and experience. Professor Gammage discusses this in depth, noting that the 'higher brain develops firstly in relation to social experience'. This means that the young brain thrives best in an atmosphere of love and consistency, and in a reliable socio-emotional environment. In practice, this means that the purposeful support of children's relationships with others will recognise that social experience is the bedrock of learning and needs to be attended to first and foremost. Equally, really tuning-in to parents will help staff to recognise the genetic traits that children have which will influence how they feel and behave at nursery.

And we know that the opposite is true: the stress that comes from poverty can shape a child's neuro-biology and lead to poorer outcomes in later life, as described by Professor Edward Melhuish in Chapter 2. The ROI, or return on investment, is higher in the early years than at any other stage of a child's school career; however it is not only the nursery or school setting which affects this: of equal, perhaps greater, importance is the home learning environment. This was one of the key findings of the EPPE project, which has helped us to know, rather than think or believe, what the optimum conditions are for a high quality learning environment to exist and to be sustainable. Early years staff can help parents to continue the nursery's work at home, by encouraging them to engage and sustain a child's piece of work when at home, by talking about the positives in the child's nursery day, and the choices they made, with the child and keyworker, and by asking parents for feedback about what the child has been doing at home – all to create a real dialogue and not merely a report about the nursery day.

What children want

Helen Huleatt reminds us in Chapter 6 that the environment needs to be for purposeful *play, not entertainment* if we are to address what children really want and need from their early years setting. And it needs to be changed sometimes, to address the needs of a new cohort of children, in order to challenge afresh the same group, or just because it is time for a change. This requires flexibility to be built-in to the design and furniture choices in the setting, and sensitivity to what significance the changes may have. Some children will respond with high stress hormone production to new organisational arrangements, a new adult present, or a change in the environment, and this kind of change may be better made when children have been observed to use the space in new ways, and so the changes are driven by the children, thus structuring the environment to optimise the experiences of children in terms of fostering their pace of development.

We heard earlier how critical the environment is to creating the right conditions for learning, and here we realise how important it is to support a change in the environment appropriately. This suggests that involving children in this change, letting them take some ownership of the change, rather than doing a 'make-over' over the weekend, is a more constructive way forward.

A report from the National Children's Bureau in 2013 showed that fifty years ago there was no difference in access to and use of open spaces and leisure facilities between advantaged and disadvantaged children. Today, there is a nine-fold difference. Social philosopher R.H. Tawney, writing in the 1960s, pointed out that 'no individual can create by his isolated action a healthy environment ... or eliminate the causes of accidents in factories or streets. Yet these are all differences between happiness and misery and sometimes, indeed, between life and death.'

Clearly, offering a safe, active and stimulating outdoor experience, both within the setting and beyond, is critical, particularly for those children who do not have such access at or from home. In terms of practice, if we are to challenge the statistics above we need to be brave about offering this experience to children, and resilient in the face of hesitation, in order to prepare young children for managing the world around them.

'It will take more than vitamin pills to secure the wellbeing of all our children', said Emeritus Professor of Family Policy in Bristol, Hilary Land. And the European Centre for Environment and Human Health, who contributed Chapter 7, would agree that health can drive a research agenda for well-being in our young children which education could recognise and adopt. Children are instinctively drawn to nature, and nature can provide the opportunity to develop *spatial awareness and relationships that form some of the building blocks of higher-level thinking.* Being free to roam is a concept that we know our children treasure; our job is to provide the safe position from which they can, and in some circumstances, this means bringing nature inside.

Playing Out is a Bristol-based not-for-profit information and advice resource for street play. It aims to increase children's safe access to informal play in residential streets through directly supporting resident-led play sessions, running workshops for parents, coordinating a national network of 'street organisers', training play and community professionals, and communicating the benefits of street play to policy makers. Playing Out events are temporary two- to three-hour after-school road closures, with one or two volunteer stewards at each road closure point. One parent said: 'This is a fantastic idea. Children have the freedom just to be outside and it also brings the community together.' The organisers say that there is a wide range of, and good interaction between, age groups, across genders and children from different schools. Children engage in both physical and creative activities including 'the longest hopscotch in the world', and simply chatting.

'Instead of being encouraged to observe and explore and develop, children are treated like geese in a foie gras farm', said George Monbiot, writing in the *Guardian*, in October 2013, about the school curriculum. And in an overview of research into outdoor education, King's College London noted that 'exploring the natural world makes other school subjects rich and relevant'.

In the UK we foster a narrow set of skills even though we all, including the government (in principle), accept the case for outdoor learning. In 2006 the Department for Children, Schools, Culture and the Environment signed a manifesto which said, 'we strongly support the educational case for learning outside the classroom. If all young people were given these opportunities we believe it would make a significant contribution to raising achievement'. But massive cuts to outdoor play facilities followed. In *Kith: The Riddle of the Childscape* (2013), Jay Griffiths claims that 'those who live in crowded flats, surrounded by concrete, mown grass and other people's property cannot escape their captivity without breaking the law'. This feeds 'stranger danger' and plays into the hands of entertainment at home and indoors, rather than purposeful play where children are free(r) to roam. Griffiths claims that our children have lost touch with their *kith*, their places, whilst seeking total dependence on *kin*, the people close to them.

Sheffield-based *Wild About Play* asked children what they most wanted to do outdoors, and they answered, to collect and eat wild foods, make fires and cook on them. There is a growing body of evidence, as illustrated by The Children's Society in Chapter 4, that happiness follows freedom. But where, and who will let them?

A plan to erect a netball hoop on a village green in Oxfordshire was blocked because 'residents didn't want to attract children'. In West Somerset an eight year old girl was stopped from cycling down her street when a neighbour complained that her wheels squeaked. In one survey, two out of three children said they liked playing outside every day, mainly to be with their friends, but 80 per cent had been told to 'come back inside'. 'Today's children are enclosed: at home, in nursery/school, in cars, by surveillance and by poverty' although time with family, friends, and outdoors are the top three happiness needs identified in UNICEF's 2011 survey. Other studies show that when children are allowed unstructured play in nature, their sense of freedom, independence and inner strength all thrive. They are not only less stressed, they are able to bounce back from stressful events more easily. But these 'unlimited' hours are constrained by diarised wall-to-wall activities arranged by adults. Maybe we need to think differently about 'free time' in our daily programmes.

These findings could change the way we think about designing and using outdoor play space in the early years. Perhaps it should not be so controlled; perhaps we should not provide prescriptive equipment that constrains imagination. Perhaps instead we should facilitate places to talk, share, allow imagination to flourish – supporting relationships between children and letting them lead their play, as we would as parents, simply keeping an eye out for danger in a garden when friends come round.

Project Wildthing reports that playing outdoors has halved in a generation. Only one in ten children regularly play in woods, streams, moorland or hillside. It cites barriers, beyond those we have already mentioned, as: lack of environmental learning in the curriculum; time-poor parents; consumerism and advertising to children; over-development and planning; and the rise of screen-time. Project Wildthing is 'marketing' nature as a playground, and as an antidote to the amount of time children spend looking at screens. Writing in the *Guardian* (1 February 2014), Zoe Williams reported from a small private hospital in London which is running a residential rehab course for screen addiction, where the youngest patient, so far, is four years old. However the game to which the child was addicted, is interactive. Children 'Skype their friends while they're playing. They're in the game with their friends as well. It's not like they sit on their own in a darkened room.' So there is an interactive quality of communication via screen.

Secure risk-taking

One of the very strong themes that all our contributors have touched on is the importance of children learning to take risks, and learning to manage risk themselves. Hopefully, we are now ready to rate the well-being of children and families above the *compensation culture*, the readiness to assign blame and seek redress, which has accompanied and guided our regulatory framework for early years education and care for so long, and was the subject of the Young Report in 2010. We are referred to a wonderful example of *secure risk-taking* in Chapter 7, where children agree between themselves when to pour more mud on a slide to make them go faster. Staff stand by for support and security. And clearly, taking risks is about being outdoors as much as inside.

The balance to be struck between encouraging risk-taking and teaching self-control is described as a consideration of the *risk-benefits* of an activity, as a positive approach to enabling children to explore and develop their curiosity. The Children's Society research on well-being tells us that control and formality imposed by adults do not score highly in relation to children's well-being; making their own choices and the autonomy the child feels, do.

A connecting theme is that we need to learn to have more confidence in children, and the importance of leaving them to their own explorations, within a secure environment. They are capable *experts in their own lives, skilful communicators, having their own rights, and 'meaning-makers'*, as shown through the work of Alison Clark and Peter Moss in *Spaces to Play* (2005). They used the *Mosaic Approach* to explore how three and four year olds handle the process of decision-making. This tool provides a methodology for placing children's perspectives at the heart of adult conversations about the services they provide. Three of their key outcomes were:

- the importance of listening to children about their environment;

- the links between listening and learning;

- the possibilities and challenges for research on listening to young children.

An important aspect of their research was to acknowledge that communicating with very young children is not limited to the spoken word – the subject of more detailed work in *Listening as a Way of Life* (Young Children's Voices Network 2004).

We need to make time to listen to children in an age-appropriate way, and include them in our plans for successful delivery of early years services, offering children the autonomy they seek.

And of course the secure environment is critical to allowing this autonomy to thrive. 'A modest amount of risk yields rewards and appropriate achievement', says Professor Gammage in Chapter 1. Making the early years setting welcoming of children's conversations and questions, helping them to learn what is dangerous, offering them the tools to assess risk, and tuning-in to each child's understanding and ability to act on what they have heard, gives reassurance to the hesitant and cools the excitement of the over-confident. Perhaps then time at the woodwork table can be looked at positively, rather than as a hazard; perhaps involving parents as the comfort in a session in the woods; perhaps staff walking along planks set on milk crates first; perhaps watching the setting manager in the office using a stapler before offering it as a mark-making tool.

What happens at home

The importance of the proven co-dependency of the learning environment at home and in the early years setting takes us to the importance of parent engagement and partnership in the child's educational development. *'The entering characteristics of the learners'*, as Bruner described what children arrive at nursery with, have driven the work of the Children's Centre and nursery and reception classes at Robert Blair School. In Chapter 5, Mark Miller goes on to share how attention to involving parents has supported them to continue their involvement further up the school, and how children have benefited. The line between the learning environments of home and school can then blur. Helping parents to reflect learning at home should then, according to research, be a way in which all settings could achieve a higher quality offer. Back in 1990, the Rumbold Report, *Starting with Quality*, said that 'Parental involvement does not merely contribute to quality but is essential if early education is to be successful.' From research, we now know this is indisputable.

Chapter 3 looks at a number of ways in which settings can encourage partnership. The main message here is that staff must try to put themselves in the shoes of parents, tune-in to their perceptions and culture, and from this starting point, develop a lasting and fulfilling partnership.

All contributors discuss, from their differing perspectives, and agree, that creating an environment where 'learning will be almost inevitable' must be our aspiration. But it doesn't stop there – implementation and maintenance of such an environment must be continuous. The issue of when children move from one room to another, by age or in relation to their own readiness, continues to be an open question. A further question is the extent to which the early years are a preparation for school. They clearly are, if the early years service is of high quality, but the evidence shows that what is actually more important for both children and parents is their well-being, their happiness, their memories of early years as an important stage in itself, and the friendships they made there. This view was celebrated in *Birth to Three Matters*, guidance from Sure Start in 2002, which sought to 'celebrate the skills and competence of babies and young children', alongside the idea that children use all their senses to communicate, the core value of the Reggio Emilia approach since its outset. But now we have the evidence, as shown in Chapter 2.

Writing in the *Observer* in December 2013, Alice Fisher talked about what parents really want for their youngest children, and how they manage the pressures upon them, concluding, as her daughter asked her 'for the umpteenth time that day, "What are you doing mummy?" Robin, I'm trying to make you happy'. And Alice Thomson in *The Times*, in July 2013, expressed her frustration about the narrowness of the curriculum: 'Before I had children I was a pail-filler.' But creativity is where Britain excels. It was the UK's creativity that brought Anish Kapoor from India, and drew the admission from Grayson Perry that it would have been difficult to flourish anywhere else. Gail Rebuck of Random House marvels at how Britain produces the best writers of children's literature, and Brian Cox points out that we produce more original research than any other country in the G8. Thomas Heatherwick, designer of the awesome 2012 Olympic cauldron, said: 'Are we going to keep pushing the idea of bowler hats or emphasise that some of the most ingenious people on this planet are based here, innovating in business, art and every possible area.'

Children need a firm foundation, but they also need to be inspired. We have to light their fires, encourage as well as cajole, so they can compete creatively, as well as academically. And Ofsted even claimed in 2014 that teachers have 'low expectations and fail to instil the right learning culture', calling it 'an unacceptable waste of human potential'.

For practitioners this means that focusing on the creative skills and experience that can be built in the early years will yield better results later, and will make for happier children – which is what parents ultimately seek. Within a culture of perceived 'school-readiness' and academic testing at a younger and younger age, this takes courage and even tenacity on the part of staff.

Practitioners

Alice Thomson went on to say that she feels it is teachers who need a new curriculum: 'they are not even showing primary school teachers how to teach children to read nor are they encouraging new recruits to be ambitious for their pupils. Concentrate now on teaching the teachers so they can teach everyone else.' A view supported by Professors Melhuish and Gammage. And it was a view put forward by Professor Cathy Nutbrown who was asked by the Department for Education to review early years education and childcare qualifications, in 2012. Her first recommendation (of nineteen), and accepted by the government, was:

> that the Teaching Agency should develop a more robust set of 'full and relevant' criteria to ensure qualifications promote the right content and pedagogical processes.

In January 2014 the National College for Teaching and Leadership responded on behalf of the Department for Education, saying it aimed to:

- improve the quality of provision, working with the Teaching Agency, by developing and promoting a highly qualified and diverse workforce in partnership with local authorities;

- continue to invest funding in graduate leadership programmes in 2012–2013 with the Teaching Agency delivering both the Early Years Professional Status and new Leaders in Early Years programmes;

- through research, look at ways in which the role of the early years provider can have a positive influence on the quality of a child's early learning in the home, which we know has significant positive benefits for children's later attainment and social behaviour.

The initiatives above then begin to steer the focus towards the adults rather than the children themselves, and support a less universal curriculum in favour of a more universal quality of teaching. Professor Gammage points out that 'research does not support any specific or universal features of a curriculum design or styles of learning that should be imposed on all children at a certain age. Ideological commitment does that.'

Research translated into practice

First published in 1998, and revised in 2003, *Quality in Diversity* was a 'framework to enable early years practitioners to think about, understand, support and extend the learning of young children from birth to the age of eight'. It was the product of a unique collaboration across the spectrum of statutory, voluntary and private sector provision, organisations and children's services. It identified the entitlements of young children as:

- *Belonging and Connecting*: to be cared for by a small number of familiar and consistent practitioners who understand and are sympathetic to their needs, who support their learning in partnership with parents and their wider community within an atmosphere of mutual respect.

- *Being and Becoming*: to be well-fed, rested, physically active, mentally stimulated, and safe from harm. To have a sense of well-being, feeling of self-worth and identity, and confidence in themselves as learners. This with the support of practitioners who have high expectations for children, offering opportunities to take risks, to experience success and failure and to reflect.

- *Contributing and Participating*: to have their own individual thoughts and choices respected, and to be encouraged to take responsibility as a member of a group within a culture of respect for diversity and equal opportunities.

- *Being Active and Expressing*: learning through all their senses through first-hand experience and play, indoors and outside. Being supported to express all their emotions and feelings.

- *Thinking, Imagining and Understanding*: having opportunities to question, learn new skills and processes, and to pursue their own interests and concerns to become critically aware, with practitioners who listen, watch, take time to value children's curiosity, and have the ability to extend children's thinking.

The entitlements were incorporated into 'the practitioner's wheel' to plan, resource and organise, support and extend learning, understand, record progress, evaluate and adapt, and to work in partnership to achieve early learning and care which meets a child's entitlements.

The contributors in this book provide us with the evidence to do what many have known for some time is right. I am grateful to them all.

References

Clark, A. and Moss, P. (2005) *Spaces to Play: More Listening to Young Children Using the Mosaic Approach.* London: National Children's Bureau.

Early Childhood Forum (1998) *Quality in Diversity.* London: National Children's Bureau.

Griffiths, J. (2013) *Kith: The Riddle of the Childscape.* London: Hamish Hamilton.

National Children's Bureau (2013) *Greater Expectations.* London: National Children's Bureau.

Nutbrown, C. (2012) *Foundations for Quality: The Independent Review of Early Education and Childcare Qualifications.* London: Department for Education.

Rumbold, A. (1990) *Starting with Quality.* London: HMSO.

Schiller, P. (2010) Early brain development research review and update. *Exchange*, Nov/Dec, pp. 26–30.

Sure Start (2002) *Birth to Three Matters.* London: Department for Education.

Tawney, R.H. (1965) *Equality.* London: HarperCollins.

Young, Lord (2010) *Common Sense, Common Safety.* London: HM Government Cabinet Office.

Young Children's Voices Network (2004) *Listening as a Way of Life.* London: National Children's Bureau.

Index

Page numbers for figures and tables are in *italics*

Index

Index

Index

WITHDRAWAL